KEYNES: ASPECTS OF THE MAN AND HIS WORK

KEYNES:
ASPECTS OF THE
MAN AND HIS WORK

*The First Keynes Seminar held at
the University of Kent at Canterbury 1972*

Edited by

D. E. MOGGRIDGE

*University Lecturer in Economics and
Fellow of Clare College, Cambridge*

ST. MARTIN'S PRESS NEW YORK

AFFILIATED PUBLISHERS: Macmillan Limited,
London – also at Bombay, Calcutta, Madras and Melbourne

Contents

List of Participants

Foreword

The University of Kent received its Charter in 1965 and the intention was that it should develop along collegiate lines. By 1968, two colleges were already functioning and a third was nearing completion. As the existing colleges had been named after T. S. Eliot and Ernest Rutherford, it was natural to turn to the social sciences for the name of the new one. Opinions were canvassed and various possibilities were discussed but to most people the name of Maynard Keynes seemed an obvious first choice. When Lord Keynes's brother, Sir Geoffrey Keynes, was approached, he warmly supported the proposal, and the name Keynes was then formally adopted by the University.

The college is pleasantly situated among the university buildings on a hill to the north of Canterbury with a splendid view of the cathedral and city. It has about 600 junior members and 100 senior members drawn from all faculties, of whom 300 junior members and a few senior members live in.

After the college had reached a fairly settled state of equilibrium, it was suggested that Lord Keynes's memory might be regularly honoured in a manner which would, at the same time, enrich the academic experience of both students and staff. Sir Geoffrey Keynes, Dr Milo Keynes and Professor Austin Robinson were consulted and all gave encouragement to the idea of a Keynes Seminar. The Faculty of Social Sciences agreed to sponsor it jointly with the college and both the Faculty and the University offered some financial support. Finally and most importantly, Macmillans undertook to publish the proceedings and to make a contribution towards meeting some of the other costs.

It was generally felt that the subject of the first seminar must be Keynes himself and the organising committee was fortunate in securing as chief speakers Sir Roy Harrod, Mr Eric White, Dr Donald Moggridge and Mr Roger Opie, each of whom has exceptional, even unique, knowledge of one or more of the different aspects of the life and work of Maynard Keynes.

The seminar took place on Friday, 10 November 1972, and attracted a large and appreciative audience. A number of Lord Keynes's relatives and friends also attended, including Mr Nicholas Dimsdale, Miss Mary Glasgow, Sir Frederic Harmer, Dr Milo Keynes and Professor Austin Robinson. Their contributions to the discussion were specially valuable and their presence and that of other visitors added much to the success of the occasion.

R. SPENCE

Session 1

INTRODUCTION
Professor W. Hagenbuch (Chairman)

We count it a quite exceptional privilege to have among us two of the elder statesmen of academic economics who knew Maynard Keynes and worked closely with him. One, Professor Austin Robinson, is in the audience, the other, Sir Roy Harrod, is our first speaker. There is not time or indeed need for me to recite the achievements of Sir Roy Harrod, his outstanding contributions to economic theory, his involvement in economic policy, his ability to write letters to *The Times*, his activities in Whitehall and Washington and in the pages of many journals, his books in areas of knowledge about as diverse as those touched by Keynes himself – all these are the fruits of a lifetime of intellectual effort and public service. During most of this time he has held the Studentship, which in the less quaint university would have been called a professorial fellowship, at Christ Church, Oxford. Perhaps his most significant achievement in relation to our seminar today is his biography of Keynes, written only a few years after Keynes's death without the perspective which a biographer would normally regard as essential, but still a masterpiece of sympathetic appraisal as refreshing to read now as it was when it was first published twenty years ago.

KEYNES'S THEORY AND ITS APPLICATIONS
Sir Roy Harrod

I feel it a great honour, as well as a great pleasure, to have been invited to give this first lecture in this place. It is an especial pleasure because Keynes himself was a dear friend of mine. He became so, I think I can say, from the moment of our first meeting. He was extraordinarily responsive and sensitive in his human relations. Thus he invited me to lunch on the basis, I should suppose, of a normal letter of introduction from Lord Runciman. I had been consulting Lord Runciman about what I should do in life. I had been offered something at Christ Church, Oxford, where economics was only just beginning; in this matter we were rather a long way behind Cambridge, where economics had been started some time before that. And so Lord Runciman said, 'Yes, I should do that, I think that's a very interesting assignment'; and he added, 'Would you like me to write you a letter to Mr Keynes?' 'Well,' I said, 'that would be marvellous.' Of course I'd read his famous works on the German reparations problems, but I'd never met him. So Runciman wrote. Keynes immediately asked me to lunch; he didn't know anything about me, and I knew no economics because we hadn't been taught any economics at Oxford. I was just a young man for whom Lord Runciman had written a letter of introduction. The lunch was in London in Keynes's flat. He welcomed me so warmly, as if he was an old friend; it really was quite astonishing. He was very sensitive, indeed I think I can say gentle, in his relations with human beings; but as soon as you got into controversy, he was no longer sensitive and gentle; he was rebarbative in the extreme, he had no mercy for those who advanced fallacious arguments, he crushed them brutally. He thought, indeed he knew, that he knew better. Fallacies made him furious, and indeed were agonising to him. He crushed you with great rudeness; his fierce manners on these occasions injured his relations with some people for life.

I believe the fact that he had such an inward fury against people who argued fallaciously had an important influence on his way of life. I haven't seen this point made before, but I think there's something in it. In private life he did not spend most of his time with economists – there was always the danger of having to suffer fools ungladly – but he spent his private life mainly among aesthetes and philosophers. When he was in London he spent a lot of time in what is commonly known as Bloomsbury – with people like Lytton Strachey, Duncan Grant and so on. The speaker just now mentioned his life style being not quite that of a hundred per cent professional economist; but I would add – I want to be perfectly fair as he would wish me to be, though he wouldn't agree with what I am going to say – he wasn't in his own person at all an aesthete. People were rather deceived when they went into his rooms and saw the modern art around them and so on, and he took an interest in many aesthetic subjects, and, of course, later in life did much to help the arts by his organisation. He took his artistic views from his great friends, people like Roger Fry and Duncan Grant, and, therefore, when he was in contact with them, he didn't keep feeling 'you're talking damn rot'; he didn't know quite enough about the subject to know whether it was rot or not. When they were talking economics he knew that they were talking rot, but when they were talking about Matisse or what not, he was prepared to acquiesce and be polite. I think that was a reason why he liked moving in a somewhat different world in his leisure time. He remained all his life a learner in such matters, so that, if somebody said something different, that didn't make him feel very furious. This is only a personal touch, and I must focus on my subject matter, which is Keynes's Theory.

Keynes was the very rare combination of a great master of economic theory – he was a great theorist in general, in logic and so on – with one who had at the same time a very fine understanding of what was actually happening in the world, the practical problems, the practicabilities of implementing a theory and so on. He was an intense realist in all those things, and that is an unusual combination. I think the realists are apt to be a little shaky when you take them on to pure theory, and the pure theorists are apt to be a little unpractical when you ask them what should be done in such and such a case. I suppose the classic example of a person who similarly combined two roles was David Ricardo, who was an absolutely first-rate theorist, but also had an understanding of what was going on in the business world.

One talks nowadays of Keynes's Theory; but he had many theories in the course of his life. We don't know whether in a very long-term horizon some of his earlier theories may not prove to be more important than what we now think of as 'Keynes's Theory' in the singular – theories which he expounded in such books as *Indian Currency and Finance*, his *Tract on Monetary Reform* and *A Treatise on Money*; these books are laced with very interesting and important theories, though what we call 'Keynes's Theory' hadn't reached fruition.

I suppose the central concept of what we call Keynes's Theory is his concept of aggregate demand. The theory is that if real aggregate demand exceeds the supply potential of the economy, you will tend to get inflationary pressures building up and inflation itself occurring. On the other hand, if aggregate demand is below the supply potential then you will have unemployment. That is, so to speak, the centrepiece of his theory. When you think of aggregate demand in Keynes's sense, you must dismiss from your mind, for the moment, at least from the forefront of your mind, questions of the money supply. Money supply does come into Keynes and plays its part, but it doesn't play a simple part, and there has to be a link between monetary theory and that concerning the level of aggregate demand. Even now, to this day, in spite of the great predominance of Keynes's thinking, there are still economists of importance who think that, if you have inflation going on, the maxim is to reduce the money supply: reduce it enough, they argue, and you will terminate inflation. That would be an un-Keynesian point of view. But, as I say, he thought that money supply, through its indirect influence on real aggregate demand, *was* important.

Keynes approached his own theory of aggregate demand by using the concept of a unit of account: this was something different from money as we ordinarily mean it. But I have a slightly different way of presenting this theory, which I think represents it fairly, however much I have to simplify.

We may consider the propensity to consume as a percentage of the consumer's income; to give it a number, let's call it 80 per cent. Suppose that consumers on the overall average tend to spend 80 per cent of their income. Then the economy requires all the time a build-up of its capital investment, whether in terms of fixed capital or circulating capital; and suppose that the investment requirements are such as to take up and absorb 20 per cent of the productive resources of the community. Then these two percentages that I have given you add up to 100, and, if they do add up to a 100, then you are in equilibrium. You haven't got over-full demand which would give rise to inflationary pressures, but you ought to have full employment if the aggregate demand is sufficient to absorb the productive resources. When I say that you have no unemployment, we must have in our minds, of course, a little footnote that in the best of all possible worlds there is bound to be a certain amount of frictional unemployment. We must admit that; but there would be full employment in the sense that frictional unemployment, etc., would be as low as possible.

Suppose, on the other hand, these two percentages add up to more than 100 then you have demand inflation, and, if they add up to less than 100 you have unemployment. I think it is the centre of Keynes's thought that there was no necessary tendency for these discrepancies to be corrected. He postulated that you could have deliberate methods of correcting them. But I think his point was that the working of a market mechanism was not such that, if you had, say, unemployment, there would be a tendency to a correction. The unemployment might or might not cause wages to fall, or to rise less than they would otherwise have done. That might indeed happen, but he did not think that that would correct unemployment. If the wages fell, to take the extreme case – we don't have falling wages very much now – then prices would follow suit; or, conversely, if wages were pushed up above the rise in the productivity of labour, then prices would tend to move up, whereas the old orthodoxy would suppose that if the market forces gave you too much or insufficient aggregate demand, the market would itself correct this, so that you would all the time have a happy and harmonious tendency to full but not over-full unemployment, subject of course to the usual frictions.

We have postulated remedies for underemployment which we now usually call monetary and fiscal policy. If there is unemployment, then you apply these; you have easier monetary policy on the part of the banking system, or you may reduce taxes, without reducing government expenditures, or increase government expenditures without increasing taxes. Those are monetary and fiscal remedies for underemployment. I think that Keynes did not think very much about the remedies for excessive demand, except when it came to advising, for instance, on economic policy in the Second World War. The fact was that during most of his working life, and of his life of creative thinking, apart from the wartime interludes, we were suffering rather nasty unemployment, even before 1929 when the great slump came, and still more after the world slump. The obvious malady of the economy was insufficient demand and underemployment; and so it was natural for him to concentrate his mind on that side of the matter rather than on the side of over-full demand. When you have over-full demand, as during a major war, then it is almost taken for granted that you will have to have, certainly in the Second World War anyhow, a rather overriding system of controls of everything, because there are many other factors in the war which make controls expedient. But you would not want to do that – and Keynes himself certainly wouldn't have wanted to do that – in peacetime, when demand is not so greatly excessive as it becomes in wartime. On the other hand, it's not quite clear by Keynesian thinking what you *ought* to do.

The orthodox remedies under the fiscal and monetary policies are to raise bank rates, have tight money and increase taxes without increasing expenditure, or reduce expenditure without reducing taxes, and so forth; but Keynes didn't go into the intricacies and specific problems arising in that situation to any great degree. I think he fully expected that after the Second World War, as after the First World War, there would be a great slump; most of the economists and experts seemed to think the same and they were all taken by surprise when such a slump did not occur at that time. They had some remedies ready at hand, but they did not have to be applied very much because in the normal course of things demand seemed to keep up fairly well.

I think it is fair to say that since the Second World War, and, unhappily, mainly since Keynes's own death, these theories of regulating aggregate demand by monetary and fiscal policies have been embodied into orthodoxy: they have been accepted. Keynes was a rebel and a revolutionary, and made proposals for remedying inflation when the orthodox, the oldfashioned orthodoxy, said all you have got to do is reduce the money supply and there would not be any inflation; there are still one or two people saying that in certain parts of the world.

But to the best of my knowledge the majority of people now are Keynesians and have been for some time. I am not only talking about economists or professors lecturing in universities; the practical people have become Keynesian, have accepted this idea that you can regulate the economy, regulate aggregate demand, by your monetary and fiscal policies. You find these ideas expressed or implied in the reports of the Federal Reserve Board, the Federal Reserve Bank of New York, the Bank of England; and even in the Bundesbank, you will find that these ideas are taken for granted; they are almost universally accepted. So that we may say that Keynes has had a very fundamental influence on economic policy in the last quarter-century.

Before Keynes this new approach had never been excogitated; but for Keynes we might have gone back to the old type of gold standard system, etc.: balance your budget on the fiscal side, and try to have a nice big surplus so as to pay off part of the National Debt. Supposing you asked whether that surplus might not be depressing to the economy and increase unemployment. Oh no, said the old orthodox school, it will not do that at all, because if you depress employment in that way, other people will increase their demand; a reduction in government demand – say the Government cuts down certain services, which would tend by itself to create unemployment – would therefore automatically cause non-government employers to increase their demand by a compensating amount. So Keynes gives a new approach to the whole matter – the system does not cure itself automatically; and, indeed, history bears out this, because all through the nineteenth century and later we had periodic bouts of substantial unemployment; it does not seem that even in the heyday of *laissez-faire* in this country the market forces were maintaining full employment. So there, I would say, is the centrepiece of Keynes's influence on the history of economic doctrine and applied economics.

To prime the point more sharply, I must add that rather different problems have been arising more recently since the days of Keynes. And I must confess that I have the idea that harm has been done by the almost automatic application of Keynesian-type remedies for evils of a different character for which they are not appropriate. For instance, supposing you have inflation, and we have had a lot of that lately, it may be due to a build-up of real aggregate demand, the tendency to consume plus investment demand becoming more than 100 per cent of what the economy can produce. That may be one cause of a build-up of inflation. But in some countries more recently we have had rather strong inflation at times when there does not seem to have been excess demand, when on the contrary there has been rather an unsatisfactorily large amount of unemployment. Here is a paradox – prices rising in a way that is injurious and objectionable, not over-full employment but a certain amount of unemployment, rather weak aggregate demand, many factories working below capacity, underemployment inside factories, unemployment outside factories. The orthodox go on to say, 'Oh you've got this inflation, you must take the appropriate measures to damp inflation, raise the bank rate, increase taxes, etc.', applying Keynesian remedies automatically to what is, basically, a different situation.

I cannot help thinking how furious Keynes would have been at this. It saddens me to think of this, because he was always so quick to adapt his mind to new problems as and when they arose; he would have seen long ago that this inflation from which we have been suffering, is not simply a symptom of what you may call Keynesian excess demand; he would have torn the skin off people who have been recently holding that a correct remedy for inflation has been for the banks to reduce their lending facilities. The inflation that we have been having is not, mind you, merely a slight inflation; I have been looking through such price histories as there are in order to assess the inflation from which we have recently been suffering – the Americans have had similar trouble. Admittedly, I do not fully trust the price histories – they have their statistical errors and so on – but I believe that it cannot be contested that the inflation in the last three years is the greatest inflation that this country has had in peacetime since the reign of Queen Elizabeth I. Here is a new problem. Here we have got inflation without excessive demand. What do we do? What is the remedy?

It would be most inappropriate for me to stand up here and tell you what Keynes would have thought. Goodness knows he would have thought of something much cleverer than I can think of. We do not know what he would have thought, but he certainly would not have thought that damping demand was the right remedy for the kind of inflation that we have got. I have searched through his writings very carefully, not long ago, for this very purpose, for the purpose of discovering anything that he had to say about what we call 'cost–push inflation', where the inflation is due to unions asking for, and being given, wage increases which, on the average, are in excess of the productivity increase of labour, of shopkeepers asking for price increases because their costs have gone up. These increases have been heavy, what we call 'cost–push inflation' being strong at a time when there has not been any excess of effective demand. I could only find one short passage in Keynes, just a couple of sentences, where he said, 'Of course the wage-earners might demand more than corresponding to their rise in productivity, might demand more and get more', and of course this would be a cause of inflation independent of those which he had been describing in his book. But he added that 'this is not a thing that is likely to occur often'. You can find those words if you search; I ought to give you chapter and verse, but I have not put down the page reference; they are there all right.

I am myself a definite advocate of what we call an 'incomes policy'. I believe there must be direct interference. I do not think it is any good saying that banks can stop inflation – saying, let them reduce the money supply. How can the poor banks reduce the money supply? What actually happens is that wage-earners get a demand granted which must raise costs of production because it exceeds the current increase of productivity; then the people who purvey the goods put this extra cost into prices. The word 'monopoly' is sometimes used for this; perhaps it is appropriate, but I am not quite sure that it is. You may say the trade unions have a 'monopoly', but it is a very imperfect sort of monopoly: I think monopoly is something that exists and is very important and has to be studied, but I think it is a somewhat different kind of phenomenon from that of the wage push, and of the wage push generating the necessity for raising prices, because the distributors, shopkeepers and so on, even the producers themselves, cannot be expected to maintain prices that have now fallen below the

cost of production plus a reasonable profit. I do not say that the
distributors are not sometimes up to a little mischief, which
adds fuel to the flames of inflation – that especially happens
when inflation has been going on and people do not see any
signs of its coming to an end; they think not only of how much
their costs have gone up, say, in the last twelve months. But
supposing that they want to print their prices in books and
catalogues and so on, they may say, 'Well, but these wages are
going on up, we see no signs that there is going to be an abate-
ment of the wage inflation, we had better stick enough into the
prices to make sure that we will not be had for mugs if the
fully expected increases are later negotiated before we get out
a new catalogue.' That is what you may rightly call wage-price
spiralling. I remember dancing round at a school camp-fire –
the school camp was organised during the First World War
for digging potatoes, because there was a food shortage at
that time – as all sang 'prices following wages and wages
following prices'. During the period of the great slump, of
course, we did not see so much of it, and the question now is
how we are going to tackle it. I do not think we can tackle it
without direct interference – not simply interference via the
quantity of money but by way of wages boards and prices
boards. They do seem to be doing this rather more effectively
in America now than here – having tribunals, boards, call
them what you will, responsible for fixing maximum price
increases. I am sure that we have got to come to that, and,
as our Chairman very kindly hinted, I had a letter in *The
Times* on this very subject yesterday.

The most difficult part of this is that of course it is a very
complex matter to fix prices: there are so many things, and
people say it's beyond the power of a tribunal to fix tens of
thousands of prices; but I think you can get around that. You
can have, say, a list of 100 standard prices, prices of absolutely
standard articles, and then people must charge those prices;
but if you can show that there is a slight improvement on the
standard article, you may add a little bit to the price. That
should be subject to inspection – not in every case, because
there are hundreds and thousands of cases – but there must be
sample inspection. You should have inspectors whose duty it
would be to sample prices and assess any deviation from the

prices in the official price list. Then we have the private citizen. There should be an easy method for the private citizen to report to an office what happened when he went into a shop to buy, shall we say, a cushion. The standard price was £4, but the shopkeeper was charging £6 for it; when he complained the shopkeeper said, 'Well, it's got those tassels on it' – but did the tassels justify a 50 per cent increase in price? The ordinary citizen should be on the lookout for those things, and the tribunal should have sample enquiries. And I think that where the offence is flagrant – if somebody puts up by 15 per cent and perhaps it ought only to be 10 per cent, that is not too bad – but where there is a large deviation from what would be justified, then I think very severe penalties should be enforced.

To come back to Keynes, and it is now rather long after his death, I cannot say what his view would have been about this wage-price spiralling, official boards and so on. He might have thought of some much better way of dealing with the problem, but I would think that, unless he had some special gadget of his own, he would be heartily in favour of the kinds of action that we are moving towards now. He would have said, 'Of course you have got to do this'; he was a great enemy of inflation and he would appreciate the point. He had sufficient quickness of thought to see that the Keynesian remedy, as we call it, and a very important remedy it has been in its own sphere, was not going to stop this wage-price spiralling. I have been talking about things which were outside Keynesian theory, because they were not within his field of thinking in the post-war period – and war is something special – and I cannot claim that he would have approved exactly of what I have been putting forward; but he would have approved – of this I am absolutely certain – of all of us trying to have fresh thoughts on this subject, trying to hammer out new ways.

The great thing about economics, whether you like it or not – and I think most economists do like it, but some non-economists if they suddenly became economists might be appalled by it –, is the ever-changing environment, and the ever-changing sets of problems to which economists are expected to give answers. They give their answers against a background of fundamental theory, and you may include in this not only the theories expounded by Marshall and Irving Fisher and so on but also the Keynesian theory of aggregate demand that is now, I think, established as part of fundamental theory. But these new problems keep cropping up; you do not quite see how the fundamental theory applies to them, or they may genuinely need additions to fundamental theory.

So we have a live subject, and I think this adds to the interest and excitement of economics. Those of you who are going to move forward and spend time on the study of economics should feel able to do so with the prospect of really making fresh contributions of significance to this old subject.

Professor W. Hagenbuch: One of the startling things about
Keynes is the way he came up with a plan at the beginning of
the last war, *How to Pay for the War.* I suppose very few
people at that time thought that the proposals which he then
put forward were the sort which we ought to envisage in order
to deal with the economic problems, including the problems of
inflation, that were likely to arise in wartime. But bearing
in mind the sort of plan that he did come up with then, as a
war measure, bearing in mind the way his mind worked in
those circumstances, I wonder whether you would agree that
if he were trying to devise a peacetime plan for our present
ills, he would in fact be very strongly in favour of the sort of
prices and incomes board which we had a few years ago?

I ask this partly because since his day one thing has happened which has changed the scene very considerably, and
that is there has become available a very large mass of statistical data and information about the working of the economy,
which was only in a very poor and elementary state in 1940–5,
and I think he would be the sort of person who would want to
seize on the availability of this material, and make use of it
as intelligently as possible, with a view to helping the regulation of the economy – not only the regulation of aggregate demand, but the regulation of all sorts of other problems. So
that with this availability of an increased amount of statistical
data I have the feeling (whether or not he'd have got on with
Mr Aubrey Jones) that he might have been rather attracted by
what the Prices and Incomes Board was trying to do (leaving
aside for the moment, how well or badly they did it), rather
than, if I may say so, the clumsy measures which we seem to be
blundering into at the present time. Do you think there's
something in that?

Sir Roy Harrod: I think the question is somewhat complex.
But first may I say that, of course, Keynes was himself very
largely responsible for the improvement of our statistics as
they have been since the war. The new statistical compilation

naturally couldn't be published during the war. But he said, 'If we're going to run this war effectively, we've got to have much better statistics,' and he encouraged the Central Statistical Office, etc., to get out for the private information of the different departments and the appropriate people much fuller statistics about the different parts of the national economy. One ought not to omit the name of the person who did the early pioneering of this kind of work, Colin Clark; but it was Keynes himself who urged the government machine to have fuller statistics.

Going back to your reference to Keynes's *How to Pay for the War*, I think I have got my chronology right. Keynes became very seriously ill more than two years before the war: he was considerably better when the war broke out, but still had to spend part of his time in bed at home, and was not able to do a full day's work. In the early days of the war it wasn't supposed that he could resume the mantle which he dropped in 1919 when he walked out of the Treasury; he couldn't go back to that sort of thing. I think I am about right, that he started by going into the Treasury once a week, or something like that, without too much detriment to his health, and then they gave him a room in the Treasury, and then, of course, he gradually became more and more enmeshed in the different kinds of planning that were proceeding, with special emphasis on thinking out plans of reconstruction on which we were getting busy in quite early days before the Americans were in the war even, because they said 'We are not going to help you with the war unless you promise to pursue policies after the war more in accord with our way of thinking' (greater freedom of trade, less import controls and so on). So he had to address his mind to that, and it was out of his thinking about that that was born his draft of the International Monetary Fund: he did a lot of work on that and had conferences with the Americans and so on, and gradually got busy.

Professor Austin Robinson: Ervin Rothbarth gave Keynes help on the statistical side, but he had in a very short time indeed reformulated the issues which he was trying to deal with in the *General Theory*, stood them on their heads and applied them to problems of inflation. He did begin to turn to inflation within weeks of the outbreak of war. In fact, the earliest version of *How to Pay for the War* was given as a Marshall Society lecture in Cambridge in October 1939.

Mr J. J. Hughes: In the debate raised among certain economists in recent years over the money supply and inflation, camps have been roughly divided between the so-called monetarists and the Keynesian followers. It seems somewhat paradoxical that the monetarists would argue that one can control all inflations by cutting back on aggregate monetary demand, whereas the Keynesians might argue that one needs new policy devices such as an incomes policy. Would you agree with this?

Sir Roy Harrod: I don't quite like this dichotomy that continues between the monetarists and the Keynesians: it is giving Keynes, so to speak, really too wide an umbrella. There *is* a distinction between the monetarists, pure and simple, and the Keynesians who believe in his theory of aggregate demand; and what I was trying to say was that on the whole Keynesians, in that sense of 'Keynesian', are in the places of power, and the monetarists are rather a sort of eccentric right-wing saying that everything can be done by controlling the money supply. I do not think the majority of people in power, whether it be the Bank of England or the Treasury or people in other places of power abroad, go back to that; I think that mostly they are Keynesians. My further point was that that is a very important problem, but it does not cover the wage-price spiralling problem. It is not a question of applying Keynesian theory, because if you have got inflation all the Keynesian theory tells you to do is to damp down a bit; that's what you do not want to do if the economy is underemployed and yet has wage-price spiralling inflation. It was the problem caused by that particular mixture that Keynes had not addressed his mind to solving. We cannot say what he would have said, but I am sure he would have looked with the greatest sympathy on those who are on this very difficult task of trying to hammer out a rational wages and prices policy by direct interference, and not hoping to do it by some sort of monetary programme alone – no monetary policy can help.

Dr A. P. Thirlwall: On the other hand is it not possible that Keynes would have been less paranoid about inflation than the current generation of policy makers and economists seems to be; that instead of interfering with the market mechanism with price controls and wage controls he might well have recommended adjustment mechanisms to compensate those who suffer the consequences of inflation?

Sir Roy Harrod: There again one cannot speak for the man who is no longer with us. I would think that he would be very intolerant of the inflation. Indeed, there's a famous passage, isn't there, in the *Economic Consequences of the Peace* about how inflation is the best way to destroy the capitalist system. He was not a narrow-minded capitalist, but he would not, I think, have liked, anyhow yet, to destroy the capitalist system. And what do you replace it with? I think he would have looked with very great hostility upon the inflation that's proceeding. That's my impression. I may be wrong. But I would guess that he would say: 'This is a great problem and we have got to think out new methods of overcoming it.'

Mr S. Oksuz: Would you say that the system of fixed exchanges was a cause of inflation?

Sir Roy Harrod: I would think the opposite. One of the things that does prompt the authorities to try and get a grip on the inflation is the fact that inflation is injuring our balance of payments. And, conversely, supposing there are other factors which bring about a deficit, some goods that you habitually import going up in world price, or goods that you habitually export being more subject to competition from perhaps Germany and so on, so that you get an adverse balance of payments and you correct that by depreciating the currency – that would certainly add fuel to the flames of inflation. Now it's all right if you have got internal deflation and it may do no harm, and Keynes would probably have approved of depreciating the currency and that would have had a two-fold effect; it may help – not necessarily – your external balance of payments and it may remove the domestic deflationary tendencies, but there can be conflicts too. But I would think – I did not really understand your question because it seemed to me to be a contradiction – that inflation and adverse balance of payments do not necessarily go together but that they are linked together the other way round.

Mr Nicholas Dimsdale: Why is there so little in the *General Theory* on the direction of principal determinants of economic growth (which has, of course, been very much the concern of economic policy in the post-war period), and particularly did Keynes see this as a natural extension of handling the problems of unemployment?

Sir Roy Harrod: I think the answer is no. I think of the timetable of it. Here was Keynes giving all his brains to the *General Theory* which is not, though it is what you call macroeconomics, dynamic. It is a general theory of how incomes and employment are determined at a given point of time. Then, poor man, he gets ill, the war breaks out, he writes this little booklet of which Austin Robinson has spoken just now, and he is entirely immersed in the war. You see, the use of growth as a regular economic concept had hardly come in before the war: it has all blossomed among various writers since the war. I don't see how Keynes can have been expected to have systematic ideas on growth; his systematic ideas related to full employment. The modern type of dynamic theory about what happens through time – he just hadn't got round to it. I am sure that he would have got round to and dealt with it very well; but the timetable of his life and death did not give him an opportunity.

Mr L. S. Krieger: You imply that you are a supporter of a prices and incomes policy and that Keynes also would have been, but when the freeze comes to an end how would you solve the problem of wages and prices pressing ever harder and making up the lost time and restarting a spiral at an even faster rate?

Sir Roy Harrod: Yes, that's a very important point. We had this trouble after the freeze of Mr Harold Wilson in 1966. We had six months' freeze which was faithfully observed; I think there were only three small cases of people breaking the law, but they were only quite small companies, and by and large throughout the country it was very faithfully observed. Then there was a period of severe restraint which went on for another six months. Well, I have worked it out and it seemed to me that in the severe restraint period the inflationary process rather went back to where it had been before 1966, but did not show any signs of making up the lost ground in the six months of total freeze. But then, after a period of severe restraint, inflation began to gallop and it was that galloping after the second of the six-month periods that was the prime cause of toppling sterling into a devaluation. Well, now, what are we going to do next? – that is what we have got to think of. That problem makes me glad to learn from the newspapers that the authorities are thinking very seriously. The freeze may be difficult to execute in all detail, but it is a simple principle for practice. How are you going to stop wage and price fixers making up lost ground when the freeze comes to an end? Well, I always say you must carry forward an incomes policy, a direct interference with wages and prices. It will not be an absolute freeze where nobody is allowed to go up at all, but it will be a period in which you have official bodies watching what is happening, in which there's a law that people are not freely allowed to push prices up. I think that is a great problem in front of the country now: we have got to face up to that. It would be too ridiculous if, after the end of this period, we suddenly fell into the kind of inflation, and worse, that we've recently been having: it would show the country as going a bit decadent.

Dr R. E. A. Poole: It seems in referring to Keynes that we cannot think what Keynes would have done if only he could have come back in our midst. Is our inability due to the lack of a rigorous intellectual tool rather than our lack of hunches or insight? What I am trying to put to you is: do we lack, as it were, the mathematics for thinking this out, for arriving at a general solution which would meet the changed situations?

Sir Roy Harrod: We do not seem to be lacking in mathematical economists; in fact, some people think they take just a little bit more of the pages of the various journals of the world than the fruits of their mathematics entitles them to have. But if it is a question of a mathematical working out of something, I am sure we have enough experts to deal with that, but fundamental theories and so on are something rather different, I mean it is not only a question of the rigorous application of a given norm to a somewhat different type of case; it may be that we need, as all scientists need at one time or another, the functioning of a creative imagination and that is something different again – something like Keynes's own theory, when having worked out everybody else's existing laws, he had a flash of insight. This is the way to look at it, as in the case of great men like Ricardo and his theory of comparative costs: the idea comes to you and then you go on and work out all the possible variations of the case.

Professor W. Hagenbuch: It all comes down to wishing we had as imaginative and exciting minds as Keynes himself, and perhaps we shall have another Lord Keynes on the horizon before long.

Session 2

INTRODUCTION
Professor W. Hagenbuch (Chairman)

We think of Keynes first as an economist, but he had, of
course, a very wide range of other interests and activities as
we've already been reminded. To mention but a few he was
a trustee of the National Gallery, he was a director of the
Bank of England, he was an ardent and very expert book
collector, and he was bursar of King's College, Cambridge;
and one could add about twenty other offices of a varied kind
to that list.

One of his most fruitful other activities, undertaken at the
height of the war in 1942, was the promotion of the Committee for the Encouragement of Music and Arts, later the Arts
Council, of which our second speaker, Mr Eric White, was for
thirty years secretary. We also have among the audience Miss
Mary Glasgow, who was at the centre of this enterprise in the
early days and who corresponded with Keynes in London,
Cambridge, Washington and other places during the war years
about the promotion of CEMA. Mr White is at present working on a history of the Arts Council which he expects to publish next year. He has already published a book on Stravinsky
and a book on Benjamin Britten and a book on English opera.
This is not his first visit to the University of Kent, he gave one
of our regular Friday evening Open Lectures in 1968 and
those who have been more than four years in this very young
university will remember his visit with pleasure.

KEYNES – ARCHITECT OF THE ARTS COUNCIL
Eric W. White

It's a great privilege for me to speak to you about Lord Keynes from my knowledge of him during the war when I was Assistant Secretary of CEMA – the Council for the Encouragement of Music and the Arts. It also gives me particular pleasure that Miss Mary Glasgow who was my guide and mentor in those early days is with us here today, and I hope she will forgive any errors or omissions in my talk.

I am at present engaged in writing a book on the Arts Council of Great Britain and I have spent some time researching the Arts Council's prehistory, which is the wartime period covered by the archives of CEMA.

My talk this afternoon will be in four parts; Keynes and the arts; the birth of CEMA; then CEMA under Keynes when he took over as Chairman in April 1942; and the planning of the Arts Council.

The first part, on Keynes and the arts, has already been touched on, because all of those who knew him were conscious, at one time or another, of his interest in the arts. It has already been mentioned that he was a great book collector and – what I think is particularly interesting in a book collector – he was a great reader too. He knew intimately many writers, personal friends in Cambridge and Bloomsbury, and valued and kept their friendship. On the side of the visual arts, he was in close touch with artists like Duncan Grant, Vanessa Bell and Roger Fry. I think Keynes's friendship with these painters brought him into close touch with contemporary trends in painting; and his attendance at the sale of the Degas collection in Paris towards the end of the First World War resulted not only in important acquisitions for the National Gallery, but also in a number of personal purchases which formed the basis of his own private collection. In 1930, in conjunction with Samuel Courtauld, he set up the London Artists Association, which guaranteed a small group of painters a modest annual income and gave them opportunities for exhibiting their work. His marriage to that popular Russian ballerina Lydia Lopokova, who I'm glad to say is still with us and celebrated her eightieth birthday a short time ago, deepened his interest in the theatre. He was closely associated with the Camargo Ballet Society which succeeded in keeping interest in ballet alive in London during that difficult inter-regnum between the dissolution of the Russian ballet after Diaghilev's death in 1929, and the tentative beginnings of the Vic-Wells Ballet Company under Ninette de Valois in 1931.

But he was also able to put into practice some of his theories about the stage, for he was directly concerned with the conception, planning, building and running of the Arts Theatre, Cambridge, which opened in 1936. Indeed, his in-terest in all matters connected with the arts was so apparent that when in the same year *The Listener* wished to launch an international enquiry into the question of Art and the State, Keynes was chosen as the opening spokesman. I want to make one quotation from this article in *The Listener** which is particularly interesting in the light of later events. After drawing attention to the view of the function of the State and of Society which had been formulated in the nineteenth cen-tury, and still prevailed in the 1930s, he wrote:

This view was the utilitarian and economic – one might almost say financial – ideal, as the sole respectable purpose of the community as a whole; the most dreadful heresy, perhaps, which has ever gained the ear of civilised people.... Poets and artists have lifted occasional weak voices against the heresy.... But the Treasury view has prevailed. Not only in practice. The theory is equally power-ful. We have persuaded ourselves that it is positively wicked for the State to spend a halfpenny on non-economic pur-poses. Even education and public health only creep in under an economic alias on the ground that they 'pay'. ... If there arises some occasion of non-economic expenditure which it would be a manifest public scandal to forgo, it is thought suitable to hand round the hat to solicit the charity of private persons.

Those I think are strong words, and remarkable in the light of what happened later.

* See Appendix 1, pp. 33–40 below, for the full text of this article.

When the war started in 1939, there was no ready plan, so far as I know, to help artists and the arts in wartime. I sometimes think that if this country had been Germany there would have been a master plan somewhere in an official desk; and all that was necessary would have been to open the drawer, pull out the plan and put it into operation. Whether the result would have been successful or not is another matter. But in this country there was no such possibility. By the end of the autumn of 1939, however, a number of people felt, perhaps a little vaguely, that something ought to be done. These were men and women of good intent. They met together, and it is startling to find how quickly their ideas moved towards fruition. The key person was Dr Tom Jones, who was then secretary of the Pilgrim Trust; and his Chairman, Lord Macmillan, happened also to be Minister of Information. The then President of the Board of Education was Lord de la Warr; and these three people met together with a few other interested persons, including W. E. Williams, Sir Kenneth Clark and Thelma Cazalet Keir. In the course of discussion it was suggested that something should be done immediately to help artists and encourage the arts in wartime. Nobody quite knew what or how; but they certainly knew quick action was vital. (I always remember that 'action' was one of the key words of Dr Tom Jones, with a rising Welsh inflection on the '-tion'.) Somebody asked how much money would be needed, and someone else suggested £5000. At that point the Pilgrim Trust representatives made their big gesture and said that if the thing was worth doing at all it was worth doing well, and they would offer a grant of £25,000.

So at the beginning of 1940 a small committee called the Committee for the Encouragement of Music and Arts (CEMA) came into existence, and that was the moment when Miss Mary Glasgow became its secretary. She was then an H.M.I. and was seconded by the Board of Education for this purpose. After only three months, that is to say by the end of March 1940, the Treasury was sufficiently interested in the work of this new Committee to agree that £50,000 should be made available for it on a pound-for-pound basis. It was upgraded to a Council, its membership slightly revised, and for the next two years, from 1940 to 1942, it had the promise of a total of £100,000 if a further £25,000 could be raised from non-government sources. At that moment it was thought that another trust, namely the Carnegie U.K. Trust, which had always shown great interest in the educational side of the arts, would step in and provide the missing £25,000. But when it came to the point, the Carnegie money was not forthcoming. Instead, the Pilgrim Trust, having acquired great belief and confidence in the work it had started, ultimately increased its contribution to £50,000, and so the whole of the Government's £50,000 could be claimed.

CEMA had no written constitution. In some ways it might be thought its terms of reference were conveyed by its title — to 'encourage Music and the Arts'. But in the course of my recent researches, I have discovered a contemporary document which I think sets forth in some detail CEMA's interpretation of its terms of reference:

(a) The preservation in wartime of the highest standards in the arts of music, drama and painting.
(b) The widespread provision of opportunities for hearing good music and the enjoyment of the arts generally for people who, on account of wartime conditions, have been cut off from these things.
(c) The encouragement of music-making and play-acting by the people themselves.
(d) Through the above activities, the rendering of indirect assistance to professional singers and players who may be suffering from a wartime lack of demand for their work.

CEMA made a quick start and in the course of the next few months there were many calls for its services. In April 1940 a monthly bulletin of activities was first issued: and it is extraordinary to look back on those early numbers and see the number and variety of the entertainments provided.

From the beginning CEMA recognised its need to co-operate with existing bodies. Many organisations were interested in music and drama, and CEMA saw to it that part of its money went to meet the salaries of organisers, advisers and other specialists in these fields. Perhaps the most interesting and the most dynamic group were the music 'travellers' who were appointed through the Rural Music Schools and were indefatigable in their work, travelling to different parts of the country, helping music to be made, and making music themselves. The boundaries between professional work and amateur work in those early days were somewhat blurred, and it was easy to move from one to the other. CEMA was so anxious to respond to requests as quickly as possible that it frequently found both the amateur and the professional sheltering under its umbrella.

The demand for entertainment varied. For instance, when the London blitz started and there were periods of heavy bombardment there was a tremendous demand for CEMA's emergency concert service. At the same time a regular series of concerts grew up in factories; and a great deal of work was done by drama companies, sometimes specially recruited, but sometimes consisting of an existing company like the Old Vic Company, touring the country and playing in war-workers' hostels. There was also an exhibition service which had been launched in the 1930s by W. E. Williams through the British Institute of Adult Education, called 'Art for the People', which CEMA supported. This was roughly the pattern of CEMA's first two years.

By the beginning of 1942 the Pilgrim Trust, having put a total of £50,000 into this operation, decided to bow out; not that they didn't believe in the value of the work, but they thought it was too important to be continued as the work of a private trust, and that if it had proved its value, as indeed it had, then it should be taken over by the Government. The result was that the Pilgrim Trust representatives on the Council resigned at the same time. This was the moment when Keynes was invited to become Chairman. I would like at this point to read a short quotation from the Annual Report of the Pilgrim Trust for 1941:

It was never CEMA's wish to foist a ready-made culture on a passive community. The demand has, in fact, presented a continual problem of supply and has dissipated scepticism about the public response to unaccustomed forms of beauty in sound and thought and design. In two years its art exhibitions have attracted more than half a million visitors, the plays given under its auspices a million and a half, the numbers of its concerts in all parts of England, Wales and Scotland almost reached 8000.

That was certainly a proud record, and such was the organisation that Keynes took over, as it were, in midstream.

To begin with, under Keynes, there were gradual policy realignments. There was a certain amount of tidying up to be done. For instance, CEMA was anxious to hand over to the Carnegie U.K. Trust the responsibility for helping amateur work in the arts, leaving itself free to concentrate on professional activities. At the same time the lines of a more permanent policy of subsidy were beginning to emerge. For the time being, the 'Art for the People' exhibition service was continued. Its organiser, W. E. Williams, who now joined the War Office as director of ABCA, still kept a close eye on its operation but there seems to have been some disagreement with Keynes over the educational implications of the work. In an article called 'The Pre-history of the Arts Council', W. E. Williams wrote: *

There was one feature of our scheme which displeased Lord Keynes, and that was our provision of guide lecturers at every major exhibition. He thought that this was wholly unnecessary, because he believed that visitors could and should do their own interpretation. There was, alas, in this great scholar and art connoisseur a streak of donnish superiority, and a singular ignorance of ordinary people. The Institute time and time again reminded him that we were not mere providers of touring exhibitions, but an educational body, with a mission to enlighten people about art. At the end of 1942 Lord Keynes persuaded CEMA to cut our grant for 1943 from the £10,000 we had asked for to £5000. Fortunately this cut was strongly resisted by Sir Kenneth Clark and myself, and Lord Keynes relented as far as to make the figure £7500.

Although this makes it sound as if the BIAE grant for these

* Included in *Aims and Action in Adult Education 1921–1971* (British and National Institutes of Adult Education, 1971).

exhibitions was cut from £10,000 to £7500, what really seems to have happened was that it was raised from £5000 to £7500, as the service continued to develop.

The next operation, a particularly important one, concerned the Bristol Theatre Royal. Keynes was extremely conscious of the general lack of suitable buildings for the arts in Great Britain, and this is stressed in many of his writings and broadcasts. So it was not surprising that he reacted with promptness and enthusiasm when his attention was drawn to the plight of the Theatre Royal, Bristol, in 1942. This beautiful little building had been in more or less continual use as a theatre since its opening in 1766, though in later years it had become something of a fleapit. Shortly after the outbreak of war it closed down, and it was only by a miracle that it was not destroyed in the course of the heavy bombing raids on Bristol. In 1941 the property was sold by auction, and its new owner was on the point of turning it into a warehouse when an appeal to save the building as a theatre was launched, some money raised, and local trustees appointed. At this point CEMA intervened. In September 1942, CEMA agreed to take a twenty-one-year lease of the theatre from the local trustees on condition they acquired the building immediately under mortgage from its owner. The lease was to be taken out in CEMA's name and the theatre would be actively managed by CEMA for the duration of the war, any profits made during the period of the lease being given to the trustees to help them pay off the mortgage and acquire the theatre as unencumbered property.

This was a startling move for an unincorporated body like CEMA to make, and Keynes was clearly conscious that he and the members of the Council had put themselves in a delicate position. Nevertheless, when the moment came for the Theatre Royal to reopen under CEMA management on 11 May 1943, he triumphantly vindicated their action in a characteristically cogent apologia printed in *The Times* under the headings 'The Arts in Wartime: Widening Scope of CEMA: Reopening of Bristol Theatre Tonight'. Here is a short quotation from that article: *

* The full text is given in Appendix 2, pp. 40–3 below.

This is a new departure for CEMA and creates a precedent in the relation of the State to the theatre which deserves to be recorded. CEMA (as bad and forbidding of name as Bancor itself!) draws its funds from the Treasury and recognises the benevolent authority of the President of the Board of Education. But it has, I am thankful to say, an undefined independence, an anomalous constitution, and no fixed rules, and is therefore able to do by inadvertence or indiscretion what obviously no one in his official senses would do on purpose.... Thus in an undisciplined moment we accidentally slipped into getting mixed up with a theatre building. Making the best of a bad job, we shall come clean tonight, without shirking publicity, in the hope of public absolution. And the precedent having been once created, it will, I hope, be officially improper not to repeat it.

That, I think, gives a characteristic picture of Lord Keynes in action. Having carefully analysed a given problem, weighed up the pros and cons and reached a considered conclusion, he was apt to act quickly, without hesitation, and to explain and justify his conduct afterwards. On this occasion his 'indiscretion' was soon forgiven. In fact, on the same day as his article appeared, *The Times* carried a fourth leader approving the course of action and offering full absolution.

Equally important in its way, though I can only refer to it quite briefly, was his interest in the Royal Opera House, Covent Garden. Here the building, which as an opera house dated back for nearly a hundred years, but which hitherto had never been the headquarters of a permanent resident opera company or ballet company, had been used by Mecca Cafés as a dance hall during the war, and it was Keynes's imaginative plan that it should be restored as a full-time opera house after the war with its own resident opera and ballet companies. It was possible to do this where ballet was concerned by promoting the Sadler's Wells Ballet Company direct from Sadler's Wells Theatre. An opera company, however, would have to be built up. Keynes was closely involved in the complicated negotiations, not only over acquiring a lease of the building itself, but also over forming the necessary company limited by guarantee to run the building and manage the opera and ballet companies; and this was a remarkable feat for a man who was so busy on other weighty matters at that time, and who nevertheless found it possible to spend so much time and thought on CEMA and its affairs.

As the war went on, it was clear that careful thought would have to be given to the future of CEMA, and about 1944 the first references occur to what might happen to it after the war. At that moment it was difficult for Keynes always to be present when such discussions took place – the period of the Bretton Woods Conference, for instance, made this impossible. A preliminary statement of intent was made on his behalf by the Secretary-General, Miss Glasgow, at a Council meeting in September 1944. Later on, when Keynes returned to London, he explained his plans in greater detail. He was anxious first of all, as an interim measure, to set up panels of music, drama and the arts to help the Council in its work. At first these panels were given executive powers; but later this was changed so they became purely advisory groups, and a separate executive committee was set up. Then came the drafting of the charter; and at that point two curious points arose.

The first concerned the title. Everyone agreed the old title must be dropped and nobody wanted a new one, the initials of which could be used to make up an artificial word. Keynes proposed that the new body should be styled the Royal Council of the Arts; but I remember that when he made this proposal there was a murmur of disapproval. Nobody on the Council seemed to like the suggestion. But once the prefix 'Royal' had been dropped, it was easy to arrive at the 'Arts Council of Great Britain', and that seemed to please everyone.

The second point occurred in connection with the aims and objects of the new institution; and here the draft wording was 'to develop a greater knowledge, understanding and practice of the arts, in particular to increase the accessibility of the arts to the public' and so on. In the course of the drafting it occurred to Keynes that, with careful wording of this clause, the Arts Council might qualify for exemption from rates under the Scientific Societies Act of 1843, where it was laid down that such exemption might be claimed by 'any society instituted for purposes of science, literature, or the fine arts exclusively, provided that such society shall be supported wholly or in part by annual voluntary contributions'. Expert opinions were canvassed on the precise meaning in this context of the expression 'fine arts', and in the end it was written into the charter. But, in the long run, the Arts Council never succeeded in getting exemption from rates, not because its aims and objects could be faulted, but because it was considered that an annual grant aid from the Treasury could not be considered as an annual voluntary contribution within the meaning of the Act.

On 12 June 1945 the Chancellor of the Exchequer (then Sir John Anderson) announced that 'impressed by the way CEMA had shown there would be a lasting need after the war for a body to encourage the knowledge, understanding and practice of the arts', the Government had decided to incorporate the Council with this object, in the name of the 'Arts Council of Great Britain'. Keynes followed this up, first with a press conference at the new Council headquarters at 9 Belgrave Square, and a few weeks later with a lively broadcast talk entitled 'The Arts Council: its Policy and Hopes'.

This brings me to the coda of this talk, where first of all I would like to stress the fact that the decision to set up the Arts Council was taken by the wartime Coalition Government, the announcement was made by the 'Caretaker Government'; and the implementation of that decision was carried out by the Labour Government. Those changes of government within a comparatively short period seemed to make no difference at all to the general feeling that the Arts Council of Great Britain was an important development and should be brought into existence forthwith.

Late in 1945, Keynes was again in America for several months. He was back in England in time for the reopening of the Royal Opera House on 20 February 1946 when the Sadler's Wells Company presented a new production of Tchaikovsky's full-length ballet *The Sleeping Beauty*. On that occasion there was a distinguished audience in the Opera House, and a slight aroma of mothballs in the foyer, auditorium and crush bar. The Royal Box was occupied by three generations of the Royal Family, and the next box but one, by Lord and Lady Keynes. Keynes suffered a slight touch of heart trouble just at the moment the Royal party arrived; but this soon passed. It was said that his wife, Lydia Lopokova, who had frequently danced the leading role in this ballet for Diaghilev during the Russian ballet season in 1922/23 at the Alhambra, took advantage of the shelter of the box, once the lights had dimmed, to discard her rather tight evening shoes in favour of a more comfortable pair of slippers. That night Margot Fonteyn scored a great triumph as Princess Aurora.

Shortly afterwards Keynes had to make a further visit to North America; and not long after his return he died of heart failure at Tilton on Easter Monday. Had he lived, an important honour would have come his way, for the King had offered him the Order of Merit; but death intervened before the award could be announced. It was also too late for his name to be written into the Arts Council charter as its first Chairman. That particular honour was to devolve on his successor, Sir Ernest Pooley. But Keynes will always be remembered as the architect of the Arts Council; and if a monument is needed, it will be found in the way 'the civilising arts of life' have subsequently flourished in this country, thanks to his wise and successful advocacy of State subsidy.

Art and the State – 1

By J. M. KEYNES

What should be the relationship between Art and the State? Mr Maynard Keynes opens here an international enquiry into this question. In subsequent articles responsible authorities will explain the policies that are followed in their respective countries

The ancient world knew that the public needed circuses as well as bread. And, policy apart, its rulers for their own glory and satisfaction expended an important proportion of the national wealth on ceremony, works of art and magnificent buildings. These policies, habits and traditions were not confined to the Greek and Roman world. They began as early as man working with his bare hands has left records behind him, and they continued in changing forms and with various purposes, from Stonehenge to Salisbury Cathedral, down at least to the age of Sir Christopher Wren, Louis XIV and Peter the Great. In the eighteenth and early nineteenth centuries the rich nobility continued in a private, self-regarding and attenuated manner what had been the office of the monarch and the State, with the Church somewhat in eclipse. But there commenced in the eighteenth century and reached a climax in the nineteenth a new view of the functions of the State and of Society, which still governs us today.

This view was the utilitarian and economic – one might almost say financial – ideal, as the sole respectable purpose of the community as a whole; the most dreadful heresy, perhaps, which has ever gained the ear of a civilised people. Bread and

* Reprinted from *The Listener*, 26 August 1936, by permission.

nothing but bread, and not even bread, and bread accumulating at compound interest until it has turned into a stone. Poets and artists have lifted occasional weak voices against the heresy. I fancy that the Prince Consort was the last protester to be found in high places. But the Treasury view has prevailed. Not only in practice. The theory is equally powerful. We have persuaded ourselves that it is positively wicked for the State to spend a halfpenny on non-economic purposes. Even education and public health only creep in under an economic alias on the ground that they 'pay'. We still apply some frantic perversion of business arithmetic in order to settle the problem whether it pays better to pour milk down the drains or to feed it to school children. One form alone of uncalculated expenditure survives from the heroic age – War. And even that must sometimes pretend to be economic. If there arises some occasion of non-economic expenditure which it would be a manifest public scandal to forgo, it is thought suitable to hand round the hat to solicit the charity of private persons.

This expedient is sometimes applied in cases which would be incredible if we were not so well accustomed to them. An outstanding example is to be found where the preservation of the countryside from exploitation is required for reasons of health, recreation, amenity or natural beauty. This is a particularly good example of the way in which we are hag-ridden by a perverted theory of the State, not only because no expenditure of the national resources is involved but, at the most, only a transfer from one pocket into another, but because there is perhaps no current matter about the importance and urgency of which there is such national unanimity in every quarter. When a stretch of cliff, a reach of the Thames, a slope of down is scheduled for destruction, it does not occur to the Prime Minister that the obvious remedy is for the State to prohibit the outrage and pay just compensation, if any; that would be uneconomic. There is probably no man who minds the outrage more than he. But he is [in] the thrall of the sub-human denizens of the Treasury. There is nothing for it but a letter to *The Times* and to hand round the hat. He even helps to administer a private charity fund, nobly provided by a foreigner, to make such donations as may be required from time to time to prevent such things as Shakespeare's cliff from being converted into cement. So low have we fallen today in our conception of the duty and purpose, the honour and glory of the State.

We regard the preservation of the national monuments bequeathed to us from earlier times as properly dependent on precarious and insufficient donations from individuals more public-spirited than the community itself. Since Lincoln Cathedral, crowning the height which has been for two thousand years one of the capital centres of England, can collapse to the ground before the Treasury will regard so uneconomic a purpose as deserving of public money, it is no matter for wonder that the high authorities build no more hanging gardens of Babylon, no more Pyramids, Parthenons, Coliseums, Cathedrals, Palaces, not even Opera Houses, Theatres, Colonnades, Boulevards and Public Places. Our grandest exercises today in the arts of public construction are the arterial roads, which, however, creep into existence under a cloak of economic necessity and by the accident that a special tax ear-marked for them brings in returns of unexpected size, not all of which can be decently diverted to other purposes.

Even more important than the permanent monuments of dignity and beauty in which each generation should express its spirit to stand for it in the procession of time are the ephemeral ceremonies, shows and entertainments in which the common man can take his delight and recreation after his work is done, and which can make him feel, as nothing else can, that he is one with, and part of, a community, finer, more gifted, more splendid, more care-free than he can be by himself. Our experience has demonstrated plainly that these things cannot be successfully carried on if they depend on the motive of profit and financial success. The exploitation and incidental destruction of the divine gift of the public entertainer by prostituting it to the purposes of financial gain is one of the worser crimes of present-day capitalism. How the State could best play its proper part it is hard to say. We must learn by trial and error. But anything would be better than the present system. The position today of artists of all sorts is disastrous. The attitude of an artist to his work renders him exceptionally unsuited for financial contacts. His state of mind is just the opposite of that of a man the main purpose of whose work is his livelihood. The artist alternates between economic imprudence, when any association between his work and money is repugnant, and an excessive greediness, when no reward seems adequate to what is without price. He needs economic security and enough income, and then to be left to himself, at the same time the servant of the public and his own master. He is not easy to help. For he needs a responsive spirit of the age, which we cannot deliberately invoke. We can help him best, perhaps, by promoting an atmosphere of open-handedness, of liberality, of candour, of toleration, of experiment, of optimism, which expects to find some things good. It is our sitting tight-buttoned in the present, with no hope or belief in the future, which weighs him down.

But before we need consider what active part the State should play, we can at least abolish the positive impediments which, as some odd relic of Puritanism, we still impose on the business of public entertainment. Of the institutions which have grown up since the War, we should most of us agree, I think – in spite of all our bickering – that the BBC is our greatest and most successful. But even the BBC must be furtive in its progress. And, incredible to relate, instead of its receiving large subsidies from the State as one would expect, an important proportion of the ten shillings which the public contribute is withheld from it as a contribution to general taxes. This was a new and difficult business requiring large-scale, costly experiments, capable of revolutionising the relation of the State to the arts of public entertainment, contributing more both to the recreation and to the education of the general public than all other mediums put together. Yet, even in its earliest and most precarious days, we considered it a proper object of taxation. On such dry husks are Chancellors of the Exchequer nourished; though probably these burdens were imposed in the spirit of fairness that requires equal injury all round. For the taxation of the BBC is only the extreme example of the general principle that we penalize music, opera, all the arts of the theatre with a heavy, indeed a crushing, tax.

Architecture is the most public of the arts, the least private in its manifestations and the best suited to give form and body to civic pride and the sense of social unity. Music comes next; then the various arts of the theatre; then the plastic and pictorial crafts – except in some aspects of sculpture and decoration where they should be the adjutants of architecture; with poetry and literature, by their nature more private and personal. While it is difficult for the State expressly to encourage the private and personal arts, fortunately they need it less, since they do not require the framework, the scale or the expense which only the organised community is able to furnish. But there remains an activity which is necessarily public and for that reason has fallen, in accordance with the aforesaid doctrine, into an almost complete desuetude – namely, public shows and ceremonies. There are a few which we have inherited and maintain, often in an antiquarian spirit, as quaint curiosities. There are none which we have invented as expressive of ourselves. Not only are these things regarded as the occasion of avoidable and, therefore, unjustifiable expense, but the satisfaction people find in them is considered barbaric or, at the best, childish, and unworthy of serious citizens.

This view of public shows and ceremonies is particularly characteristic of the western democracies, the United States, France, ourselves and our Dominions. I suggest that it is proving a weakness not to be ignored. Are there any of us who are free from strong emotion when an occasion arises for all the people dwelling in one place to join together in a celebration, an expression of common feeling, even the mere sharing in common of a simple pleasure? Are we convinced that this emotion is barbaric, childish or bad? I see no reason to suppose so. At any rate, the provision of proper opportunities for the satisfaction of this almost universal human need should rank high in the arts of government; and a system of society which unduly neglects them may prove to have done so to its peril. The late King's Jubilee, originally planned by the authorities on a very modest scale, provided an extraordinary example of the craving of a public, long deprived of shows and ceremonies, especially outside London, for an opportunity to collect in great concourses and to feel together. These mass emotions can be exceedingly dangerous, none more so; but this is a reason why they should be rightly guided and satisfied, not for ignoring them. This side of public life is one which we have so long neglected that we should scarcely know how to set about reviving it in a contemporary spirit, significant and satisfactory to this generation. For this reason we shall read with particular interest the succeeding articles of this series in which those who are concerned with these manifestations in certain European countries will tell us something of their methods, both in this respect and in the general relations of the State to art, entertainment and ceremony.

The revival of attention to these things is, I believe, a source of strength to the authoritarian states of Russia, Germany and Italy, and a genuine gain to them, just as the lack of it is a source of weakness to the democratic societies of France, the United States and Great Britain. In so far as it is an aspect – and it partly is – of an aggressive racial or national spirit, it is dangerous. Yet it may prove in some measure an alternative means of satisfying the human craving for solidarity. Much of the public ceremony and celebration now in fashion abroad strikes us, when we read about it, as forced and artificial, an occasion for bombastic oratory, and sometimes extremely silly. But we should like to know more. Here is an immemorial function of the State, an art of government regarded at most times as essential, which we have largely discarded as fit only for children and savages. Are we right to do this? This question, together with the wider problem of the relationship of the State to the Arts, is the subject of these articles.

Our present policies are a just reflection of a certain political philosophy. I suggest that this philosophy is profoundly mistaken and that it may even, in the long run, undermine the solidity of our institutions. We shall only change our policies if we change the philosophy underlying them. I have indicated an alternative point of view. Let me conclude with two illustrations, as examples of what might follow from a change of mind – one for the preservation of what we have inherited, the other for the enlargement of what we shall transmit.

(1) There should be established a Commission of Public Places with power to issue an injunction against any act of exploitation or development of land or any change or demolition of an existing building, where it considered such act to be contrary to the general interest, with power to grant compensation to the extent that was fair in the circumstances, but not as of right. Similarly where the repair or maintenance or acquisition of a place or building was in the general interest,

the Commission should have power to meet any part of the expense.

(2) Initial preparation should be made, so that some plans will be ready and available to ward off the next slump for the embellishment and comprehensive rebuilding at the public cost of the unplanned, insalutary and disfiguring quarters of our principal cities. Taking London as our example, we should demolish the majority of the existing buildings on the south bank of the river from the County Hall to Greenwich, and lay out these districts as the most magnificent, the most commodious and healthy working-class quarter in the world. The space is at present so ill used that an equal or larger population could be housed in modern comfort on half the area or less, leaving the rest of it to be devoted to parks, squares and playgrounds, with lakes, pleasure gardens and boulevards, and every delight which skill and fancy can devise. Why should not all London be the equal of St James's Park and its surroundings? The river front might become one of the sights of the world with a range of terraces and buildings rising from the river. The schools of South London should have the dignity of Universities with courts, colonnades and fountains, libraries, galleries, dining-halls, cinemas and theatres for their own use. Into this scheme there should be introduced the utmost variety. All our architects and engineers and artists should have the opportunity to embody the various imagination, not of peevish, stunted and disillusioned beings, but of peaceful and satisfied spirits who belong to a renaissance.

I affirm that there can be no 'financial' obstacle to such achievements, provided that the labour and the material resources are available. It is the relative abundance of the latter which should determine the pace at which we decide to work. It is not in itself advisable to aim at speed. The best buildings are planned and erected slowly, subject to patient criticism and evolving under the architect's eye. We should move, in London and in our other cities, at the rate made possible by the state of employment in other directions. If this condition is observed, the scheme must necessarily enrich the country and translate into actual form our potentialities of social wealth.

The Arts in Wartime

Tonight, at the Theatre Royal, Bristol, Dame Sybil Thorn-dike, in the character of Mrs Hardcastle, speaks a new prologue before *She Stoops to Conquer*, with the company of the Old Vic, is played once again on the boards where Garrick's prologue was spoken in 1766. In 1766 the Theatre Royal was a new and, as it proved, an enduring experiment in the planning and aesthetics of the theatre. For it was the first to be built in this country with the seats rising from the pit tier above tier in a semi-circle. In these latter days, with its beauties undimmed, the oldest theatre we have was, like St Paul's, preserved by extraordinary chance from bombs and fire amidst surrounding desolation.

But in this peculiar country so much luck was not enough by itself to save a national monument – even when it was of rare beauty, when it echoed the voices of Siddons, Kemble, Kean, Macready, Irving and Ellen Terry, and when it was still competent and useful to provide fresh delight to new multitudes. A year ago, saved from the enemy without, it was to be pulled down to make room for a warehouse. By timely action the citizens of Bristol opened an appeal fund and appointed trustees. That also was not enough to furnish and restore the place as the home of the living stage. So the Council for the Encouragement of Music and the Arts (CEMA), a body now wholly supported out of State funds, took over from the trustees the costs of equipment and the daily tasks of management, hoping in due season to hand the enterprise back to Bristol, unencumbered with debt, for local administration.

* Reprinted from *The Times*, 11 May 1943, with the permission of the editor.

This is a new departure for CEMA, and creates a precedent in the relation of the State to the theatre which deserves to be recorded. CEMA (as bad and forbidding a name as Bancor itself!) draws its funds from the Treasury and recognises the benevolent authority of the President of the Board of Education. But it has, I am thankful to say, an undefined independence, an anomalous constitution and no fixed rules, and is, therefore, able to do by inadvertence or indiscretion what obviously no one in his official senses would do on purpose.

> So, when Sir Kingsley told us that for staving
> Defeat, there was no saving grace like saving,
> We took him at his word, and, strictly loyal,
> For England's honour, sav'd — the Theatre Royal.

Thus in an undisciplined moment we accidentally slipped into getting mixed up with a theatre building. Making the best of a bad job, we shall come clean tonight, without shirking publicity, in hope of public absolution. And, the precedent having been once created, it will, I hope, be officially improper not to repeat it.

The functions of CEMA are evolving rapidly, and an account is soon out of date. In wartime an important part of them is to provide hundreds of factory concerts, to carry the drama to mining villages and war hostels where many of the audience see the living stage for the first time, to assist holidays at home and the provision of entertainment in parks and public places. With the aid of Mr W. E. Williams, who has been a great pioneer, we circulate through the British Institute of Adult Education large numbers of exhibitions of pictures and screen displays on such motives as 'The Rebuilding of Britain', having an educational aim and providing a worthy distraction for the mind. Last week a ballet company working in association with us (I pay a tribute to Mme Rambert) played to the wild delight of 3000 workers within the walls of a Midlands factory.

All our companies must perform their quota of such national service for the enlargement of public content in time of war. But we also seek, and increasingly, to aid all those who pursue the highest standards of original composition and executive performance in all branches of the Arts to carry their work throughout the country, and to accustom the great new audiences which are springing up to expect and to approve the best. The leading symphony orchestras and string orchestras, most of the painters, and a large majority (I think I can now say) of the opera, ballet and drama companies in the country pursuing a serious artistic purpose are working in occasional or continuous association with us. Our policy is to be satisfied with their work and purpose in general terms, and to leave the artistic control with the companies and individuals concerned; and they, with the plays, pictures and concerts they offer, may be as many and as various as there are individuals of genius and good will.

The life of this country in the realm of the Arts flows more strongly than for many a year. Our most significant discovery is the volume of popular demand. Apart from what we deliberately provide gratis or at nominal cost for wartime reasons, the money required to support so much activity is negligible. It is impossible today to offer in any large town in England a masterpiece worthily presented and to lose much money, if there is any building capable of holding the audience which assails the box-office. It was not always so. We are capitalising, I fancy, the success of the BBC (which we grumble against as against one we love) in stimulating and raising the popular taste.

But the lack of buildings is disastrous. The theatres, concert halls and galleries well suited to our purpose, taking the country as a whole, can be counted in a few minutes. That is where money will be wanted when in due time we turn to construct instead of to destroy. Nor will that expenditure be unproductive in financial terms. But we do have to equip, almost from the beginning, the material frame for the arts of civilisation and delight. If it is thought fit to preserve after the war any part of the organisation and experience that CEMA, which is on a temporary basis, will have acquired, this, I believe, is the fruitful line of development. If with State aid the material frame can be constructed, the public and the artists will do the rest between them. The Muses will emerge from their dusty haunts, and Supply and Demand shall be their servants. To begin the good work, let us build temples for them as our memorial to the gallant endurance of Plymouth and Coventry and the rest, and of old London herself. Or to use language clearer to the departments concerned – let us give this bottleneck a high priority. At any rate, do not let us lose what we already have. So hold us well justified at Bristol. I have already quoted from the brilliant prologue (far, far better than Garrick's) which Mr Herbert Farjeon has written for this occasion. In another passage he has a couplet which CEMA, and indeed all of us, might take as a motto:

> Making it our endeavour, first and last,
> To serve the present and deserve the past.

The Arts Council:
its Policy and Hopes

In the early days of the war, when all sources of comfort to our spirits were at a low ebb, there came into existence, with the aid of the Pilgrim Trust, a body officially styled the 'Council for the Encouragement of Music and the Arts', but commonly known from its initial letters as CEMA. It was the task of CEMA to carry music, drama and pictures to places which otherwise would be cut off from all contact with the masterpieces of happier days and times: to air-raid shelters, to wartime hostels, to factories, to mining villages. ENSA was charged with the entertainment of the Services; the British Council kept contact with other countries overseas; the duty of CEMA was to maintain the opportunities of artistic performance for the hard-pressed and often exiled civilians.

With experience our ambitions and our scope increased. I should explain that while CEMA was started by private aid, the time soon came when it was sponsored by the Board of Education and entirely supported by a Treasury grant. We were never given much money, but by care and good housekeeping we made it go a long way. At the start our aim was to replace what war had taken away; but we soon found that we were providing what had never existed even in peace time. That is why one of the last acts of the Coalition Government was to decide that CEMA with a new name and wider opportunities should be continued into time of peace. Henceforward we are to be a permanent body, independent in constitution, free from red tape, but financed by the Treasury and

* Reprinted from *The Listener*, 12 July 1945, by permission.

ultimately responsible to Parliament, which will have to be satisfied with what we are doing when from time to time it votes us money. If we behave foolishly any Member of Parliament will be able to question the Chancellor of the Exchequer and ask why. Our name is to be the Arts Council of Great Britain. I hope you will call us the Arts Council for short, and not try to turn our initials into a false, invented word. We have carefully selected initials which we hope are unpronounceable.

I do not believe it is yet realised what an important thing has happened. Strange patronage of the arts has crept in. It has happened in a very English, informal, unostentatious way – half-baked if you like. A semi-independent body is provided with modest funds to stimulate, comfort and support any societies or bodies brought together on private or local initiative which are striving with serious purpose and a reasonable prospect of success to present for public enjoyment the arts of drama, music and painting.

At last the public exchequer has recognised the support and encouragement of the civilising arts of life as a part of their duty. But we do not intend to socialise this side of social endeavour. Whatever views may be held by the lately warring parties, whom you have been hearing every evening at this hour, about socialising industry, everyone, I fancy, recognises that the work of the artist in all its aspects is, of its nature, individual and free, undisciplined, unregimented, uncontrolled. The artist walks where the breath of the spirit blows him. He cannot be told his direction; he does not know it himself. But he leads the rest of us into fresh pastures and teaches us to love and to enjoy what we often begin by rejecting, enlarging our sensibility and purifying our instincts. The task of an official body is not to teach or to censor, but to give courage confidence and opportunity. Artists depend on the world they live in and the spirit of the age. There is no reason to suppose that less native genius is born into the world in the ages empty of achievement than in those brief periods when nearly all we most value has been brought to birth. New work will spring up more abundantly in unexpected quarters and in unforeseen shapes when there is a universal opportunity for contact with traditional and contemporary arts in their noblest forms.

But do not think of the Arts Council as a schoolmaster. Your enjoyment will be our first aim. We have but little money to spill, and it will be you yourselves who will by your patronage decide in the long run what you get. In so far as we instruct, it is a new game we are teaching you to play – and to watch. Our wartime experience has led us already to one clear discovery: the unsatisfied demand and the enormous public for serious and fine entertainment. This certainly did not exist a few years ago. I do not believe that it is merely a wartime phenomenon. I fancy that the BBC has played a big part, the predominant part, in creating this public demand, by bringing to everybody in the country the possibility of learning these new games which only the few used to play, and by forming new tastes and habits and thus enlarging the desires of the listener and his capacity for enjoyment. I am told that today when a good symphony concert is broadcast as many as five million people may listen to it. Their ears become trained. With what anticipation many of them look forward if a chance comes their way to hear a living orchestra and to experience the enhanced excitement and concentration of attention and emotion, which flows from being one of a great audience all moved together by the surge and glory of an orchestra in being, beating in on the sensibilities of every organ of the body and of the apprehension. The result is that half the world is being taught to approach with a livelier appetite the living performer and the work of the artist as it comes from his own hand and body, with the added subtlety of actual flesh and blood.

I believe that the work of the BBC and the Arts Council can react backwards and forwards on one another to the great advantage of both. It is the purpose of the Arts Council to feed these newly-aroused and widely-diffused desires. But for success we shall have to solve what will be our biggest problem, the shortage – in most parts of Britain the complete absence – of adequate and suitable buildings. There never were many theatres in this country or any concert-halls or galleries worth counting. Of the few we once had, first the cinema took a heavy toll and then the blitz; and anyway the really suitable building for a largish audience which the modern engineer can construct had never been there. The greater number even

of large towns, let alone the smaller centres, are absolutely
bare of the necessary bricks and mortar. And our national
situation today is very unfavourable for a quick solution.
Houses for householders have to come first.

And so they should. Yet I plead for a certain moderation
from our controllers and a few crumbs of mortar. The rebuilding of the community and of our common life must
proceed in due proportion between one thing and another.
We must not limit our provision too exclusively to shelter and
comfort to cover us when we are asleep and allow us no con-
venient place of congregation and enjoyment when we are
awake. I hope that a reasonable allotment of resources will be
set aside each year for the repair and erection of the buildings
we shall need. I hear that in Russia theatres and concert-halls
are given a very high priority for building.

And let such buildings be widely spread throughout the
country. We of the Arts Council are greatly concerned to de-
centralise and disperse the dramatic and musical and artistic
life of the country, to build up provincial centres and to pro-
mote corporate life in these matters in every town and county.
It is not our intention to act on our own where we can avoid
it. We want to collaborate with local authorities and to encourage local institutions and societies and local enterprise to
take the lead. We already have regional offices in Birming-
ham, Cambridge, Manchester, Nottingham, Bristol, Leeds,
Newcastle-on-Tyne, Cardiff and Edinburgh. For Scotland and
for Wales special committees have been established. In Glasgow, in particular, the work of the Citizens Theatre is a
perfect model of what we should like to see established every-
where, with their own playwrights, their own company and
an ever-growing and more appreciative local public. We have
great hopes of our new Welsh Committee and of the stimulus
it will give to the special genius of the Welsh people. Certainly in every blitzed town in this country one hopes that
the local authority will make provision for a central group of
buildings for drama and music and art. There could be no
better memorial of a war to save the freedom of the spirit of
the individual. We look forward to the time when the theatre
and the concert-hall and the gallery will be a living element
in everyone's upbringing, and regular attendance at the

theatre and at concerts a part of organised education. The return of the BBC to regional programmes may play a great part in reawakening local life and interest in all these matters. How satisfactory it would be if different parts of this country would again walk their several ways as they once did and learn to develop something different from their neighbours and characteristic of themselves. Nothing can be more damaging than the excessive prestige of metropolitan standards and fashions. Let every part of Merry England be merry in its own way. Death to Hollywood.

But it is also our business to make London a great artistic metropolis, a place to visit and to wonder at. For this purpose London today is half a ruin. With the loss of the Queen's Hall there is no proper place for concerts. The Royal Opera House at Covent Garden has been diverted to other purposes throughout the war. The Crystal Palace has been burnt to the ground. We hope that Covent Garden will be re-opened early next year as the home of opera and ballet. The London County Council has already allotted a site for a National Theatre. The Arts Council has joined with the Trustees of the Crystal Palace in the preparation of plans to make that once again a great People's Palace.

No one can yet say where the tides of the times will carry our new-found ship. The purpose of the Arts Council of Great Britain is to create an environment to breed a spirit, to cultivate an opinion, to offer a stimulus to such purpose that the artist and the public can each sustain and live on the other in that union which has occasionally existed in the past at the great ages of a communal civilised life.

Miss Glasgow: For me, who was with him at this time, Mr White has made it all come alive in a most extraordinary way. The prologue I would like to add is this. Mr White suggested that Lord Keynes became Chairman of the Arts Council – of CEMA rather – in March 1942 and that was that. But it is my strong view that he had always intended to be just that, and when I say always I mean since the very beginning of the setting up of CEMA.

In March 1941 he had as his guests in Cambridge (you have said he was the chairman of the trustees of the Arts Theatre, Cambridge) the Pilgrim Players, headed by Martin Brown. He had them there for a week or a fortnight, I can't remember which. It was stated in the programme for the Players that the trustees were happy to offer the facilities of the Arts Theatre, Cambridge, and all the takings of their season as at present in the hope that they would be able to use it for further work up and down the country in wartime. Now having done that, which was an exciting, rather romantic gesture, Keynes then wrote to the Secretary of CEMA to tell us what he had done, and to suggest that it might be a jolly good thing if CEMA, too, was to give the Pilgrim Players some money – which they immediately did. At this time I was the lowest form of life at CEMA: I was the secretary in the back room. Lord Keynes – Mr Keynes as he then was – told one of his friends that if he wanted something he always believed in approaching the bottom, and he did just that; he wrote to the lowest form of life, and of course the lowest form of life was immensely flattered. Keynes also put in a little barb in his letter. He said: 'I think it's time your Council began thinking more seriously about the professional arts, you've given far too much time and money to the amateurs, come off it.' And then he followed up – I can't remember if it was by letter or by telephone – with a request for me to go and see him. Well, you can imagine I was faint with veneration and terror mixed. I went to Gordon Square (and here I remember Sir Roy was saying that he'd had this illness and was pretty frail at the time) and I remember being received by him, lying most gracefully on a daybed, propped up with terrific magnificent snow-white pillows with crimson velvet curtains hanging behind him. At that moment he expounded his belief that State money should be given to the support of the professional arts and that all this music-making and play-acting should fall a little bit into the background in any long-term future of State aid to the arts.

Professor Robinson: I wonder whether Mr White stressed quite enough Lydia's part in all of this. I saw this happening mostly in relation to the foundation of the Arts Theatre in Cambridge, built, of course, largely – partly at least – in order to give Lydia an opportunity to perform. It was opened by the Vic-Wells Ballet, followed by an Ibsen season in which Lydia took a large part. I've always believed that in relation to all these things he was doing, it was Lydia's care for them, it was Lydia's interests, and Lydia's wisdom about a great many of the things of the theatre which were allied to Maynard's administrative capacity, but the fire in his belly about much of this came from Lydia, I would think.

Mr White: It hardly calls for an answer from me, but I think too as far as I could judge that this was probably the flame that nurtured his interest in the arts. Naturally, from the point of view of CEMA and the Arts Council, I saw this largely through committee meetings and matters of administration at which, of course, he was enormously skilful; but it was perfectly clear that a man who was so busy in spite of being in physical ill health much of the time, would not have given so much of his mind and thought and body to this work if he had not truly believed it was important. I think that belief did come, enormously, to him through love for Lydia, and his admiration of her as an artist, and for the way she opened up to him so many aspects of theatrical life.

Professor Spence: After reading Sir Roy's book and listening to what has been said this afternoon, one wonders how much Keynes owed to his education. I believe that his family were not wealthy but they were, of course, established academics in Cambridge. He had the advantage of being educated at

Eton and I'd be interested to know whether either Sir Roy or Mr White would care to comment on the relative importance of his education and his innate personal ability. He had tremendous brilliance and confidence: he penetrated into the Treasury at a very young age, and he was able to write a work which brought a major change in ideas and attitudes after the First World War. These things, together with his appreciation of music, literature and the arts and his powerful, brilliant style of writing seemed to come very easily and quickly. It would be interesting to hear your comments on the importance of his background and education.

Mr White: I find that very difficult to answer myself, I don't think I can altogether. I don't know whether Sir Roy can?

Sir Roy Harrod: I don't think the man owed very much in the particular things that you've listed to his family background. They were quite simple inartistic people. He owed a great deal, I have no doubt, to his father on the side of logic and that sort of thing – accurate thinking. He owed a great deal to his mother on the side of getting things done; she knew how to get things done in the city council or whatever it might be. But I would not say that from either of those two he got much insight into things artistic. I think that it was something born within him, but it also came partly from other sources, especially, of course, from his friends at Cambridge, the Apostles and so on. He mixed in and he found it easy to circulate with people who were very artistic and quite different from the ordinary sort of academic and more academically trained people. So there I would say that on the technical side of his philosophy and certain parts of economics his mind was made accurate by his father's accuracy, and on the dynamic side he was influenced by his mother's character, but on the artistic side I think he really got it from his friends.

Mr White: Might I add a brief coda to that? I had the feeling at CEMA and the Arts Council that the fact that he had founded and was so closely concerned in the running of the Cambridge Arts Theatre was of enormous help to him. This was a practical side of work and administration in the arts which he had been partly responsible for himself, and which he watched very carefully. I think he learned from this and was able to apply the lessons to many of the problems, the other artistic problems that he met in the Arts Council. It always seemed to me that the fact that in the background here was his own concern in the running of the Cambridge Arts Theatre (which brought in the arts generally and was not only a theatre – it brought music in almost as much as drama, and also brought in films) gave him an extraordinarily actual and practical approach.

Session 3

INTRODUCTION
Professor M J. C. Vile (Chairman)

The interpenetration of politics and economics and their dependence on each other hardly needs emphasis, especially at a time when the political consequences of Keynesian economics are a matter of everyday concern. We are therefore lucky, I think, this afternoon to have two speakers who can approach these problems from perhaps rather different but none the less closely related positions. Dr Moggridge, Fellow of Clare College, Cambridge, is at present one of the joint editors of *The Collected Writings of John Maynard Keynes* which are in the course of publication and has written books on British monetary policy between the wars and the problem of the return to gold in 1925, a study of the formulation of economic policy. Mr Opie, Fellow of New College, Oxford, is an economist who has written widely and broadcasts frequently on economic policy and political affairs generally.

KEYNES: THE ECONOMIST
D. E. Moggridge[*]

As analyses of what Keynes is supposed to have said or meant and assessments of his contributions to modern economics are legion, my contribution to this afternoon's discussions will be along somewhat different lines. To my way of thinking,

[*] I should like to thank Professors E. A. G. Robinson, Lord Kahn, G. C. Harcourt and Mr R. Wallace for helpful advice on an earlier draft. Of course, none of them bears any responsibility for the final product.

before we can begin to understand Keynes the economist through his writings or assess his contribution, it is necessary first of all to get, at least partially, inside the man behind the books or articles under consideration: one must become aware of his habits of thought, his methods of working, his views as to the nature of economic enquiry, the just society and the like. Thus as an introduction to your own consideration of the economics of Keynes, I will attempt to sketch out the working economist in Keynes.

Exactly how one does this presents something of a problem. For Keynes did not leave posterity documents similar to Robbins' *Autobiography of an Economist*[1] or his *The Nature and Significance of Economic Science*,[2] Harrod's 'Scope and Method of Economics'[3] or Mrs Robinson's *Economic Philosophy*,[4] to mention only four possible introductions to the thought of three economists. Rather his views on the nature of economics, along with the clues to his mental processes as an economist are scattered over ten books, several hundred articles and the roomful of papers from which Elizabeth Johnson and I are attempting to distil the Royal Economic Society's *Collected Writings of John Maynard Keynes*. However, from this mass of material, I think one can begin to get that understanding of Keynes the working economist essential to any appreciation of his work. For there, in drafts, in correspondence, in comments on the work of others and in various asides, one begins to catch a flavour of the man – and of the economist.

But still, where does one begin? Perhaps the most useful point of departure is an appreciation of the intellectual background from which Keynes emerged – i.e. an appreciation of the environment of what might be called 'Cambridge economics'. For most certainly Keynes was a product of this world and, consciously or unconsciously, steeped in its traditions. For he was the son of a Cambridge economist, known to subsequent generations of economists as the author of *The Scope and Method of Political Economy*,[5] he grew up in a world which included the discussions of Cambridge economists; he corrected the proof sheets of the posthumous third edition of Sidgwick's *Principles of Political Economy* at eighteen;[6] and he was a student of both Marshall and Pigou.

Thus, at the outset, one should look at the views of this circle or school.

At first blush, there is one distinctive characteristic in the work of this founding generation of modern Cambridge economics which is shared by many of its successors. In its work, taken as a whole, the founding generation clearly regarded economics as a moral science. Although it did accept a theoretical distinction between positive and normative arguments, in practice it saw that the two were closely intermingled.[7] As Keynes put it to R. F. Harrod in 1938 during a discussion of the latter's 'Scope and Method of Economics' and Tinbergen's *Statistical Testing of Business Cycle Theories: A Method and its Application to Investment Activity*:[8]

Economics is a science of thinking in terms of models joined to the art of choosing models which are relevant to the contemporary world. It is compelled to be this, because, unlike the typical natural science, the material to which it is applied is, in too many respects, not homogeneous through time. The object of a model is to segregate the semi-permanent or relatively constant factors from those which are transitory or fluctuating so as to develop a logical way of thinking about the latter, and of understanding the time sequences to which they give rise in particular cases.

Good economists are scarce because the gift of using 'vigilant observation' to choose good models, although it does not require a highly specialised intellectual technique, appears to be a very rare one.

In the second place, as against Robbins, economics is essentially a moral science and not a natural science. That is to say, it employs introspection and judgements of value....

I also want to emphasise strongly the point about economics being a moral science. I mentioned before [in the previous letter] that it deals with introspection and with values. I might have added that it deals with motives, expectations, psychological uncertainties. One has to be constantly on one's guard against treating the material as constant and homogeneous. It is as though the fall of the apple to the ground depended on the apple's motives, on whether it is worthwhile falling to the ground, and whether the ground wanted the apple to fall, and on mistaken calculations on the part of the apple as to how far it was from the centre of the earth. . . .

One aspect of the 'moral scientific' nature of Cambridge economics was a commitment to certain practical social ends. This affected the nature of what the economist did – and what he regarded as worthwhile in the work of others. Keynes noted this clearly in his essay on Marshall:[9]

He had an inclination to undervalue those intellectual parts of the subject which were not *directly* connected with human well-being or the condition of the working classes or the like, although *indirectly* they might be of the utmost importance, and to feel that when he was pursuing them he was not occupying himself with the Highest ... When his intellect chased diagrams and foreign trade and money there was an evangelical moraliser of an imp somewhere inside him that was so ill-advised as to disapprove. [Italics in the original]

Keynes saw this as something of a defect in Marshall, although the defect of a great quality, 'his immense disinterestedness and public spirit'.[10] Others, however, certainly saw the same tendencies in Keynes. As Pigou said, inevitably comparing him with Marshall:[11]

Both were alike in their single-minded search for truth and also in their desire that the study of Economics should serve, not as a mere intellectual gymnastic, but directly, or at least indirectly, for the forwarding of human welfare ... In his *General Theory* there are some, as I think, unwarranted strictures on parts of Marshall's *Principles*. But that in no wise meant that he had ceased to be a firm disciple of the 'Master'.

Similarly Schumpeter in assessing Keynes the economist wrote:[12]

The higher ranges of mathematical economics are in the nature of what is in all fields referred to as 'pure science'. Results have little bearing – as yet, in any case – upon practical questions. And questions of policy all but monopolised Keynes's brilliant abilities. He was much too cultivated and much too intelligent to despise logical niceties. To some extent he enjoyed them, to a still greater extent he bore with them; but beyond a boundary which it did not take him long to reach, he lost patience with them. *L'art pour l'art* was no part of his scientific creed.

Austin Robinson and Harrod have also noted Keynes's extremely practical bent as an economist.[13] Thus we have here an essential clue to our understanding of Keynes the economist: his immense practicality and almost complete absorption in questions of policy.[14] It was this characteristic that lay behind his choice of emphasis in handling theoretical problems in the *General Theory*. As he told J. R. Hicks in 1935: 'I deliberately refrain in my forthcoming book from pursuing anything very far, my object being to press home as forcibly as possible certain fundamental opinions – and no more.'[15] In fact, Keynes's ideal economist was in many respects a practical, if right-thinking, technician – a dentist, to borrow one of his phrases.[16] And in his own work as an economist Keynes might almost be classified in this respect as an extraordinary civil servant. For he used traditional methods of analysis for policy problems until they broke down, and then proceeded to fashion new tools to fill in the gaps – no more. Keynes saw the economist as providing an essential element in the 'possibility of civilisation' – hardly a grand role, but an essential one.[17]

This intense practicality coloured all of Keynes's working life as an economist. It came out very clearly in his comments on the work of others – as a reader of manuscripts for publishers,[18] editor of the *Economic Journal*, unofficial civil servant or general reader. Thus he might reject what he recognised as a competent article for the *Journal* with a comment to his assistant editor: 'I do not find it [in this case an article on tax shifting] interesting or really relevant to anything that matters.'[19] A typical reply to another potential contributor runs as follows: 'I do not doubt that a serious problem will arise when we have a combination of collective bargaining and full employment. But I am not sure how much light the kind of analytical method you apply can throw on this essentially political problem.'[20] In fact, it is clear from the editorial correspondence for the *Journal* that Keynes, while reflecting current trends in economic thought, attempted to keep its contents directed to the things that mattered, and on occasion he set higher standards for more formal or mathematical pieces which he thought could conveniently go elsewhere.[21]

During the Second World War, Keynes's practical interests and his strong belief in the usefulness of economics brought him to solicit, favour and print *Journal* articles on wartime and post-war problems in preference to more theoretical fare.[22] This approach accounts for his attempt, in a way rather unusual within the context of the traditions of the British Civil Service, to draw extensively on those inside the official machine, for he 'could see no advantage and much disadvantage in post-war [and other] problems being debated secretly without the benefit of collective criticism and judgement'.[23] The results are clear in the *Economic Journal* of the period, particularly in the Meade–Fleming symposium on the pricing policies of state-owned industry, which arose directly from contemporary official discussions[24] and the Clauson paper on Colonial Currency Boards which had its origins in an internally-circulated document.[25]

Again, during the Second World War, we find Keynes's 'practical' tendencies as an economist coming to the fore in official discussions; he kept theory in its place. Thus in connection with a discussion of an Economic Section paper entitled 'Quotas vs. Depreciation' he wrote:[26]

I did not say that you should not be attached to the price system. (I share your attachment.) I said you should not be deceived by it. I still feel that the consequences you attribute to exchange depreciation may be based on being deceived as to how the price system works out in practice as compared with the way it should work out on certain theoretical assumptions. And perhaps you will not complain of my being a little bit confirmed in my suspicion by your frank confession that, like D. H. R[obertson], you are influenced by an unscientific bias of preference!

Or again in discussing Lerner's idea of functional finance:[27]

I still say, however, that functional finance is an idea and not a policy; part of one's apparatus of thought but not, except highly diluted under a considerable clothing of qualification, an apparatus of action. Economists have to try to be very careful, I think, to distinguish the two.

These last two extracts from letters lead us on to another characteristic of Keynes the economist. For they hint at another hallmark on everything he attempted. Keynes approached all problems with a mind that attempted to get to the fundamental bases of an argument or a system. One sees this repeatedly in his editorial comments or articles submitted to the *Journal*,[28] in his discussions of the work of others[29] and in his repeated attempts to get the arguments of the *General Theory* just right.[30] Only this habit of mind can, I think, explain the almost inordinate care he took over the definitional chapters of the *General Theory* during 1934–5.[31] Keynes used the same approach in his 1940–6 Treasury work, making it his business to challenge assumptions, often with magisterial derision.[32] One Treasury economist-colleague from this period characterised his many contributions to Treasury discussions as follows:[33]

I would say that what dominated his approach to any matter was a philosophy – a habit of mind. He was always ready and eager to make the best possible synthesis of the available data, thence to carry this reasoning where it might lead him and to *offer* (repeat offer) conclusions. But unlike many, he never forgot the fundamental importance of premises and the invalidity of good reasoning on incomplete premises (Propn. 2.21 of *Principia Mathematica* refers). So while it was usually impossible to attack his reasoning he was always ready and willing to revise his conclusions if his premises were attacked and could be shown to be wrong or imperfect. He could be pretty difficult in resisting attack, but if it succeeded – never mind whether from the office boy, or the office cat for that matter – he had the tremendous capacity of always being willing to start afresh and re-synthesise.... So the continuing value, as it seemed to me, of so much of his work in that time was in provoking critical examination and analysis of the facts of the situation – the premises.

Surely this Second World War comment covers other areas and periods of Keynes's life as a working economist. Certainly it is this approach which lies in the background to his rather unsympathetic reaction to Tinbergen's *A Method and its Application to Investment Activity*, the first volume of the League of Nations' series, Statistical Testing of Business Cycle Theories.[34] Keynes had commented on an early draft of the manuscript for the League, but took on a review only at the request of his assistant editor, Austin Robinson.[35] When he submitted it, he was uneasy that the review might be 'probably a waste of time' and not 'within my competence',[36] but it provides a useful piece of additional evidence to his approach to economic matters. For from the beginning of the review, Keynes was concerned with the premises of Tinbergen's argument. His questions, which displayed some ignorance of the methods involved,[37] concerned interdependencies, lags, measurability, statistical usage, the appropriate use of models, etc. The article, and the subsequent comment on Tinbergen's reply (which incidentally often told Keynes that his questions were answered in a book unavailable to him at the time of writing the review, hardly a suitable defence), also make it clear that Keynes was not unsympathetic to Tinbergen's enterprise.[38] How could he be, when at the time he wrote the review he was encouraging statistical research in Cambridge in what, after a war-imposed gap, became the Department of Applied Economics in Cambridge? Keynes was solely concerned with the assumptions and premises of Tinbergen's method. After their difficulties at modelling econometrically the behaviour of advanced industrial economies in recent years, economists surely would not cavil at much of the following comment to Roy Harrod stimulated by Tinbergen's earlier draft:[39]

> My point about Tinbergen is a different one. In chemistry and physics and other natural sciences the object of experiment is to fill in the actual values of the various quantities and factors appearing in an equation or formula; and the work when done is once and for all. In economics that is not the case, and to convert a model into a quantitative formula is to destroy its usefulness as an instrument of thought. Tinbergen endeavours to work out the variable quantities in a particular case, or perhaps in the average of several particular cases, and he then suggests that the quantitative formula so obtained has general validity. Yet in fact, by filling in figures, which one can be quite sure will not apply next time, so far from increasing the value of his instrument, he has destroyed it. All statisticians tend this way . . .
>
> The point needs emphasising because the art of thinking in terms of models is a difficult – largely because it is an unaccustomed – practice. The pseudo-analogy with the physical sciences leads directly counter to the habit of mind which is most important for an economist to acquire.

It was this seriousness concerning assumptions and premises that underlay much of the purpose of his *General Theory*. Keynes attacked his 'classical' contemporaries, not because most of them disagreed with him on policy proposals in connection with the slump,[40] but because he believed that their policy recommendations were inconsistent with the premises of their theory. One must remember that he singled out Professor Robbins with a backhanded compliment as almost alone among contemporary economists in maintaining a consistent scheme of thought, 'his practical recommendations belonging to the same system as his theory'.[41] Thus in 1937, after the publication of Pigou's *Capitalism and Socialism*,[42] Keynes could write to Richard Kahn:[43]

> Many thanks for sending me a copy of the Prof's new book. As in the case of Dennis [Robertson], when it comes to practice, there is really extremely little between us. Why

do they insist on maintaining theories from which their own practical conclusions cannot possibly follow? It is a sort of Society for the Preservation of Ancient Monuments.

Keynes was not in fact attacking *most* of his fellow economists for being 'classical' in their policy recommendations. Indeed in most countries there was a high degree of agreement on such matters.[44] Rather, he was concerned with the inconsistency he saw between their theoretical premises and their policy conclusions. He believed that this inconsistency was a source of weakness in economists' influence on policy which on occasion led to unnecessary and unhelpful public controversy. Thus he attempted to get his professional colleagues to reconsider their premises.[45] Whether he fully succeeded or not is still a matter for debate.[46]

With a knowledge of this characteristic of Keynes's approach one can understand more clearly many of his contributions to public discussion. In his *Economic Consequences of the Peace* he was questioning the assumptions concerning the nature of the European economic system implicit in the Peace Treaties of 1919. In *The Economic Consequences of Mr Churchill* he questioned the authorities' assumptions concerning the international economic position of Great Britain in 1925 and the mechanism of adjustment to a higher value of sterling in terms of foreign currencies. Similarly, *The End of Laissez Faire* is a discussion of social assumptions. Perhaps Keynes's great influence as a moulder of public opinion came from his clear efforts to lay bare with clarity the implicit assumptions of others for public scrutiny rather than to quibble over details.

However, despite Keynes's emphasis on the premises of arguments and his care in the development of many of his own ideas, it would be misleading to leave you with a picture of Keynes's working as a remorseless logician. For, if anything, Keynes was the most intuitive of men. Austin Robinson[47] has emphasised this most strongly in his selection of what must surely be introspective passages in Keynes's biographical essays on Malthus, Marshall and Newton.[48] The Marshall passage, written in 1924, is perhaps the most instructive in this connection:

But it was an essential truth to which he held firmly that those individuals who are endowed with a special genius for the subject and have a powerful economic intuition will often be more right in their conclusions and implicit presumptions than in their explanations and explicit statements. That is to say, their intuitions will be in advance of their analysis and their terminology. Great respect, therefore, is due to their general scheme of thought, and it is a poor thing to pester their memories with criticism which is purely verbal.

The intuitive nature of Keynes's thought processes comes out clearly at many points in Keynes's work as an economist. Occasionally, in his discussions with possible contributors to the *Economic Journal* he would make the nature of his thought-processes explicit and write, 'You have not expressed it [a mathematical argument] in a way in which I am able to bring my intuition to bear clearly.'[49] Similarly in the development of what became the *General Theory* one can see from students' lecture notes, correspondence and fragments of drafts that Keynes had intuitively grasped most of the essentials of his system as early as 1932. However, it took another three years of redrafting and discussion to clothe that intuition in what he regarded as a technically adequate form for his practical purposes.[50] For with Keynes, intuition represented an early but essential stage in the act of creation. Hard, systematic, careful work then went into developing the scheme of thought for the consumption and persuasion of the world at large.

As the reference to Marshall indicates, however, Keynes believed that intuition always ran ahead of analysis to some extent. Moreover he believed, one suspects from his own experience, that the author–reader relationship depended on intuition as much as formal logic. This idea was more completely developed in a draft dating from the 1934 preface for the *General Theory*:[51]

It is, I think, of the essential nature of economic exposition that it gives not a complete statement, which even if it were possible, would be prolix and complicated to the point of obscurity, but a sample statement so to speak, out of all the things which could be said, intended to suggest to the reader the whole bundle of associated ideas, so that, if he catches the bundle, he will not in the least be confused or impeded by the technical incompleteness of the mere words which the author has written down, taken by themselves.

This means, on the one hand, that an economic writer requires from his reader much goodwill and intelligence and a large measure of co-operation; and, on the other hand, that there are a thousand futile, yet verbally legitimate, objections which an objector can raise. In economics you cannot convict your opponent of error – you can only convince him of it.

It is this point of view, a result of Keynes's own habits of thought and work, that explains his unusually fierce reaction to Professor Hayek's lengthy critical review of the *Treatise on Money*, [52] when in a reply to criticism of his own Keynes turned on Hayek's most recent work as follows:[53]

> The reader will perceive that I have been drifting into a review of Dr Hayek's *Prices and Production*. And this being so, I should like, if the editor will allow me, to consider this book a little further. The book, as it stands, seems to me to be one of the most frightful muddles I have ever read, with scarcely a sound proposition in it beginning with page 45, and yet it remains a book of some interest, which is likely to leave its mark on the mind of the reader. It is an extraordinary example of how, starting with a mistake, a remorseless logician can end up in Bedlam.

For when one looks at Keynes's copy of Hayek's review, the most heavily annotated article in the surviving copies of Keynes's journals, one finds Keynes wrote: 'Hayek has not read my book with that measure of "goodwill" which an author is entitled to expect of a reader. Until he does so, he will not know what I mean or whether I am right.'[54] Perhaps a similar reaction to what he believed to be unsympathetic criticism marred (from Keynes's side) the once pleasant Robertson–Keynes relationship in the 1930s.[55]

Thus far, I have concentrated on Keynes's mental processes – his habits of thought and his characteristic method of attacking problems. However, no attempt to understand Keynes the economist would be complete without some reference to his views of what we often call 'the policy process' and 'the good society'. For with his emphasis on the practical, his almost desperate concern to influence policy and his numerous exercises in persuasion (both 'private' and public) they are vital for an appreciation of his economic writing.

As a working economist looking out on the world of his time, Keynes was very much the rationalist – perhaps too much so. His whole life was a constant campaign, in his eyes, against 'madmen in authority', 'lunatics' (a very common word in his vocabulary) and others who acted according to prejudices and rules of thumb rather than reason carefully applied to an evolving situation – whether in making peace treaties, commercial policy proposals, exchange rate decisions or mundane administrative decisions. His assessment of Mr Beaumont Pease, Chairman of Lloyds Bank, in 1924 illustrates this:[56]

Mr. Pease ... deprecates thinking, or – as he prefers to call it – 'the expenditure of mental agility'. He desires 'straightly to face the facts instead of to find a clever way round them', and holds that, in matters arising out of the quantity theory of money, as between brains and character, 'certainly the latter does not come second in order of merit'. In short, the gold standard falls within the sphere of morals or of religion, where free thought is out of place.

Similarly, although on another level, he wrote of a 1941 State Department paper:[57]

The bulk of this paper, which is a very able one within its own limitations, is a dogmatic statement of the virtues of laissez-faire in international trade on lines familiar forty years ago, most of which is true, but without any attempt to state theoretically or to tackle practically the difficulties which both the theory and the history of the last twenty years have impressed on most modern minds. Mr. Pasvolsky [the paper's author] *looks* like Rip Van Winkle and evidently *is*, in fact, he! [italics in the original]

Keynes always believed that 'a little clear thinking' or 'more lucidity'[58] could solve almost any problem. Throughout his life, he used every means available to encourage it. The methods he chose reflected his view of the forces shaping public opinion and of the policy process.[59] Keynes always carried with him 'the presuppositions of Harvey Road',[60] one of the most important of which was that the government of Britain would remain in the hands of an intellectual élite. This élite of civil servants, politicians, journalists and the like, was open to two influences – rational persuasion and public opinion. In Keynes's view, the élite played a dual role: for not only was it privy to its own 'inner opinion' but it also formed part of the 'outside' opinion in public speeches, newspapers and the like. Through its links with outside opinion, the élite could, and in Keynes's opinion should, influence the public at large. Keynes also saw the forces of changing economic events as perhaps the most important other long-run determinant of opinion among the public at large. In his view, persuasion could lead to an articulation of this outside opinion, as well as alter inner opinion. Thus Keynes in his impatience to short-cut normal long-run tendencies and influence events in the direction he desired, saw his exercises in persuasion as performing a dual role. For they would remove and undermine old prejudices, highlight likely trends and generally prepare the ground among the public at large, so that the élite once persuaded could lead rather than follow, guide rather than obfuscate. In such a situation, private meetings with Chancellors of the Exchequer, broadcasts and articles in the *Daily Mail* each had their role.

In his attempts at persuasion, Keynes had great faith in rationality. He believed that individuals, both inside and outside, could rationally appreciate the appropriateness of a line of policy. Proper persuasion could wear down prejudice and open previously unexploited areas of choice. As he wrote to T. S. Eliot on the possibilities of a successful policy of full employment:[61]

It may turn out, I suppose, that vested interests and personal selfishness may stand in the way. But the main task is producing first the intellectual conviction and then intellectually to devise the means. Insufficiency of cleverness, not of goodness is the main trouble. And even resistance to change as such may have many motives besides selfishness.

This credo, plus his own great faith in his personal powers of persuasion, provides an essential clue to Keynes's behaviour as an economist. For example, it certainly gave rise to his faith in the possibilities of economic management of all kinds and often made him its most optimistic advocate. It also lay behind his approach to the 1945 American Loan negotiations – his belief that the Americans on his masterly exposition of the case would see the sense of Justice[62] and offer Britain a large gift to ease the transition to peacetime conditions in the interests of the post-war world – and his advocacy of a technical, civil service, management for the clearing union and the IMF. It also possibly lurked behind his frequently expressed, if rather naïve, view that a rational appreciation of a situation would lead very often to a single policy proving acceptable to opinion generally.[63] Overtones of this view appear in the *General Theory*, his wartime Treasury papers and elsewhere.[64] However, towards the end of his life, Keynes at times accepted that his presumption of rationality, with its consequential effects on his approach to the policy process, was a reflection of his early beliefs. As he told a group of friends in 1938:[65]

As cause and consequence of our general state of mind [when young] we completely misunderstood human nature, including our own. The rationality which we attributed to it led to a superficiality, not only of judgement, but also of feeling ... I still suffer incurably from attributing an unreal rationality to other people's feelings and behaviour (and doubtless to my own, too). There is one small extraordinarily silly manifestation of this absurd idea of what is 'normal', namely an impulse to *protest* – to write a letter to *The Times*, call a meeting in the Guildhall, subscribe to some fund when my presuppositions as to what is normal are not fulfilled. I behave as if there really were some

authority or standard to which I can successfully appeal if
I shout loud enough – perhaps it is some hereditary vestige
of a belief in the efficacy of prayer. [Italics in the original]

However Keynes did not espouse causes merely because he
opposed stupidity and error and wanted to increase the scope
for rationality in human affairs. For he clearly had a view of
the good society. This view, although less based than in the
cases of Jevons and Marshall on widespread observation and
experience of the lives of all manner of men,[66] and although
possibly too overlaid with many of the 'presuppositions of
Harvey Road' and Bloomsbury, has proved remarkably in-
fluential. For Keynes was what Lambert has called a 'neo
liberal', perhaps one of the first.[67] By his own admission Keynes
lay at the 'liberal socialist' end of that broad spectrum of political and social thought that runs from von Mises and his
successors leftwards.[68] Keynes had, from the beginning, naturally rejected *laissez faire* in its dogmatic form, as had Marshall
and Pigou before him. From the beginning he emphasised
the essential fragility of the economic order which others took
to be natural and automatic and emphasised the need for
conscious management.[69] However, from the mid-1920s Keynes
went further and actively developed a clear 'social and political philosophy'. Then in a series of essays and speeches he
provided a statement of his political and social creed, which
with minor amendments was to guide him for the rest of his
life.[70] Along with other essays, they clearly demonstrate that
Keynes was an extremely bad 'party man', using political
parties as vehicles for his ideas and detaching himself with
ease when they proved unhelpful. They also demonstrate that
he regarded contemporary capitalism as a necessary, but not
permanent evil – a system which delivered the goods reason-
ably efficiently, safely channelled potentially disruptive energies into relatively less harmful channels, and, owing to the
role of convention, was capable of considerable reform without affecting performance, while accumulating the capital
necessary to 'solve' the economic problem.[71] At all times it was
a means, albeit a morally distasteful one, to an end, and he did
not believe that 'there is any economic improvement for which
revolution is a necessary instrument'.[72] In the organisation of

contemporary capitalism, the exact areas for state action or intervention, the agenda of government, Keynes saw as pragmatically chosen. For Keynes the rationalist had no fear of bureaucrats and officials, provided they all held the appropriate moral outlook. 'Dangerous acts can be done safely in a community which thinks and feels rightly, which would be the way to hell if they were executed by those who think and feel wrongly.'[73] As he stated his political credo in 1939:[74]

> The question is whether we are prepared to move out of the nineteenth-century *laisser faire* state into an era of liberal socialism, by which I mean a system where we can act as an organised community for common purposes and to promote social and economic justice, whilst respecting and protecting the individual – his freedom of choice, his faith, his mind and its expression, his enterprise and his property.

It was from this position that he was prepared to experiment, with his perhaps over-optimistic view of the powers of persuasion, to release men from the yoke of drudgery and privation, to allow them to enjoy the finer things of life, both material and spiritual and to prepare the world for 'the economic possibilities of our grandchildren' when 'we shall once more value ends above means and prefer the good to the useful'.[75] Thus it is not surprising that he should use a talk, 'Art and the State', to propose a programme of massive public works to make the south bank of the Thames from County Hall to Greenwich 'the equal of St. James's Park and its surroundings'.[76] For Keynes always wanted to put and keep the economic problem in perspective, behind other matters of greater and more permanent significance.

Thus we have come full circle – back to Keynes's view of the practical ends of his work as an economist. Of course, given the limited time at our disposal, we do so with only a partial picture of this man for whom economics provided just one outlet for his energies and his intellect – even his 'recreations' were remarkably creative by most standards.[77] However, I hope I have provided you with some of the background necessary to an understanding of this rather unique economist – one of the few who left his own world much the better for his passing through it.

NOTES

1. London: Macmillan, 1971.
2. London: Macmillan, 1932; second edition 1935.
3. *Economic Journal*, XLVIII (191), September 1938.
4. London: C. A. Watts, 1962.
5. London: Macmillan, 1890; later editions, 1897, 1904, 1917.
6. London: Macmillan, 1901.
7. See for example Keynes, *Scope and Method*, 3rd. ed., pp. 60-3; A. Marshall, 'The Old Generation of Economists and the New', in *Memorials of Alfred Marshall*, ed. A. C. Pigou (London: Macmillan, 1925), esp. pp. 310–11; Robinson, *Economic Philosophy*, p. 74.
8. Where quotes from Keynes's correspondence or books or essays are from works already published in the *Collected Writings of John Maynard Keynes* (London: Macmillan, 1971–   ) reference will be made to these as follows: *Collected Writings*, volume number, page. In this case the reference is to *Collected Writings*, XIV, pp. 296–7, 300.
9. *Collected Writings*, x, p. 200.
10. *Collected Writings*, x, p. 201.
11. A. C. Pigou, 'The Economist', in *John Maynard Keynes 1883–1946* (Cambridge: King's College, 1949), p. 21.
12. J. A. Schumpeter, 'Keynes, the Economist (2)', *The New Economics: Keynes' Influence on Theory and Public Policy*, ed. S. E. Harris (London: Dobson, 1948), p. 74.
13. See for example E. A. G. Robinson, 'John Maynard Keynes 1883–1946', *Economic Journal*, LVII (225), March 1947, p. 10; R. F. Harrod, *The Life of John Maynard Keynes* (London: Macmillan, 1951), p. 332.
14. This is not to suggest that Keynes, the man, was always as practical. Keynes had a relatively low opinion of the purely intellectual possibilities of economics. For higher intellectual pleasure he turned to other fields, in particular philosophy. On other occasions he turned to ancient history – drafts of a work on ancient monetary history, almost on the scale of a fellowship dissertation, survive for example from the period during which he was writing his *Treatise on Money* – and to book collecting and the arts. His mind had several dimensions, not always kept in separate compartments – as potential contributors to *Economic History* and the *Economic Journal* on such subjects as the economic reform of Solon and as Newton the economist discovered to their dismay. By comparison, today's leading economists often seem like one-dimensional men.
15. Letter to J. R. Hicks, 21 June 1935.
16. *Collected Writings*, IX, p. 332.
17. Harrod, *Life*, p. 194.
18. One of these clearly refutes Mrs Robinson's approving reference to Gerald Shove's remark 'that Maynard had never spent the twenty minutes necessary to understand the theory of value' (*Economic Philosophy*, p. 79). The book in question is Mrs Robinson's *The Economics of Imperfect Competition* (London: Macmillan, 1933) for

which he acted as referee. See letter to H. Macmillan, 25 November 1932.

19. Letter to E. A. G. Robinson, 22 August 1941.

20. Written in April 1944.

21. Letter to R. G. D. Allen, 22 August 1937.

22. Only on these grounds, plus, perhaps, Keynes's friendship with the author, could the *Economic Journal* print Samuel Courtauld's article, 'An Industrialist's Reflections on the Future Relations of Government and Industry', LII (205), April 1942.

23. Letter to E. A. G. Robinson, 22 August 1941.

24. 'Price–Output Policy of State Enterprises', *Economic Journal*, LIV (215–16), December 1944.

25. G. L. M. Clauson, 'The British Colonial Currency System', *Economic Journal*, LIV (213), April 1944; letter to Clauson, 16 October 1943.

26. Letter to J. M. Fleming, 22 April 1944.

27. Letter to F. Machlup, 25 October 1944.

28. See, for example, his discussion of Harrod's 'First Essay in Dynamic Theory', *Collected Writings*, XIV, pp. 321–50.

29. Here the classic case must be J. R. Hicks' *The Theory of Wages* (London: Macmillan, 1932; 2nd edition 1963). Keynes read the book in manuscript for Macmillan and reported to them that he was out of sympathy with its method and assumptions. He recognised the book as being 'fairly good of its kind' and likely 'to meet with extremely favourable reviews in many quarters if it were published'. His lack of sympathy resulted from his belief, growing at this time as he was writing the *General Theory*, that the traditional theory of wages could not handle problems of disequilibrium such as unemployment. However, as he admitted, the same criticisms could be applied to many reputable economists, including Professor Pigou. Therefore he asked Macmillan to ask for a second opinion from D. H. Robertson (letter to Harold Macmillan, 27 April 1932). Hicks takes up the story from there in his second edition (*Theory of Wages*, p. 307).

30. See *Collected Writings*, XIII, ch. 5.

31. For in the papers one finds evidence of much more redrafting in these sections than elsewhere. See *Collected Writings*, XIII, ch. 5.

32. Thus in his July 1944 Cabinet Paper, 'The Problem of our External Finance in the Transition', Keynes bluntly attacked the foundations of official policy:

> The government's post-war domestic policy is based on the assumption that we shall be able to import all the raw materials and foodstuffs necessary to provide full employment and maintain (or improve) the standard of life. This assumption is, at present, a blind act of faith. No means of making it good has yet been found. There has never been a more distinguished example of 'It will all come right on the day'. This memorandum is an attempt to support faith with good works. . . .

He was to spend the last two years of his life doing so, in a series of brilliant, if ultimately ineffective, papers arguing for consistency and sense in policy.

33. Letter from Sir Frederic Harmer.

34. Keynes's review and the surrounding correspondence appear in *Collected Writings*, xiv, pp. 285–320.

35. Letter to E. A. G. Robinson, 6 March 1939.

36. Letter to E. A. G. Robinson, 4 August 1939.

37. This ignorance has led Professor Klein to regard the review as one of Keynes's 'sorriest professional performances' (L. R. Klein, 'The Life of John Maynard Keynes', *Journal of Political Economy*, LIX (5), October 1951, p. 450). While Klein is often right at the technical level, some of the important methodological questions raised by Keynes in the review and surrounding correspondence have not been answered.

38. Letter to O. Lange, 10 April 1940.

39. *Collected Writings*, xiii, pp. 299–300.

40. See for example D. Winch, *Economics and Policy: A Historical Study* (London: Fontana, 1972), chs 6–9; J. R. Davis, *The New Economics and the Old Economists* (Ames: University of Iowa Press, 1971).

41. *Collected Writings*, vii, p. 20 n.

42. London: Macmillan, 1937.

43. *Collected Writings*, xiv, p. 259.

44. See note 40.

45. *Collected Writings*, vii, p. xxi.

46. See A. Leijonhufvud, *On Keynesian Economics and the Economics of Keynes* (London: Oxford University Press, 1968). In this connection Professor Davis's study of the policy proposals of predominantly Chicago economists (*The New Economics and the Old Economists*) is of more than passing interest. Perhaps because many American economists agreed with Keynes on policy, they tended to underplay or miss the actual argument of the *General Theory* concerning assumptions, thus creating a neo-classical synthesis including Keynesian economics but removing many of the awkward questions raised in the economics of Keynes.

47. E. A. G. Robinson, *John Maynard Keynes: Economist, Author, Statesman* (London: Oxford University Press, 1971), pp. 8–9.

48. *Collected Writings*, x, pp. 107, 211 n., 365.

49. Letter to O. Lange, 10 April 1940.

50. See *Collected Writings*, xiii, ch. 5. At this point, I should draw the reader's attention to Keynes's consequent use of 'the Cambridge didactic style' in presenting his arguments – a style which follows logically from his concerns as an economist. See L. E. Fouraker, 'The Cambridge Didactic Style', *Journal of Political Economy*, lxvi (1), February 1958.

51. *Collected Writings*, xiii, pp. 469–70.

52. F. A. Hayek, 'Reflections on the Pure Theory of J. M. Keynes', *Economica*, xi (33) and xii (35), August 1931 and February 1932.

53. *Collected Writings*, XIII, p. 252.

54. *Collected Writings*, XIII, p. 243.

55. See *Collected Writings*, XIII and XIV.

56. *Collected Writings*, IX, p. 188.

57. Minute of 5 January 1942.

58. *Collected Writings*, IX, pp. 335, 373.

59. In what follows I have drawn heavily on *Collected Works*, III, ch. 1, and IX, as well as on discussions with Austin Robinson.

60. Harrod, *Life*, pp. 183, 192–3.

61. 5 April 1945.

62. Justice was one of the three possible routes Keynes saw towards a post-war settlement. It involved a large gift from the U.S. to Britain to ease the transition to a liberal post-war world. The other two routes he named Starvation Corner and Temptation. For background details see D. E. Moggridge, 'From War to Peace', *The Banker*, CXXII (558 and 9), August and September 1972.

63. Thus Keynes could write in a minute on full employment dated 14 February 1944, 'Theoretical economic analysis has now reached a point where it is fit to be applied ... [With adequate statistics] it will all be obvious and as clear as daylight with no room left for argument.' Similarly in 1939, he could imply that all the best people in British politics were liberals like himself, who, if they realised it, would reduce the unreality of much party-political activity ('Democracy and Efficiency', *New Statesman and Nation*, 28 January 1939, p. 122).

64. Only in the *Tract* did Keynes seem less catholic in his solutions (*Collected Works*, IV, ch. 4).

65. *Collected Writings*, X, p. 448.

66. Both Marshall and Jevons made some attempt to study and to understand working-class life and had come to political economy through such study (*Collected Works*, X, p. 171; *Papers and Correspondence of William Stanley Jevons*, edited by R. D. Collinson Black and R. Könekamp, I (London: Macmillan, 1972), p. 17). In Keynes's case, there is no record of any such attempt beyond his interest in the agricultural workers on College estates after 1928. Thus, although he wished to improve the lives of ordinary people, Keynes's approach to the problem of doing so had its roots in a more abstractly based moral concern to remove waste and absurdities rather than in a first-hand knowledge. Whether this mattered, looking at his work as a whole, is, of course, open to discussion. For a view that it did see E. Johnson, '*The Collected Writings of John Maynard Keynes*: Some Visceral Reactions', a paper read to the 1972 annual meeting of the Association of University Teachers of Economics.

67. P. Lambert, 'The Social Philosophy of John Maynard Keynes', *Annals of Collective Economy*, XXXIV (4), October–December 1963, pp. 484–6.

68. 'Democracy and Efficiency', p. 123.

69. See for example *Collected Writings*, I, pp. 70–1; II, ch. 2.

70. The bulk of these appear in *Collected Writings*, IX.

71. *Collected Writings*, IX, p. 294; VII, pp. 375–7; IX, p. 329.

72. *Collected Writings*, IX, p. 267.

73. Letter to F. A. Hayek, 28 June 1944. 'Dangerous acts' included using the power of the state on occasion to crush private interests, as in the case of his recommendation to the Chancellor in the spring of 1920 for a 10 per cent bank rate – a recommendation he said he would give again in the same circumstances as late as 1942. See *Collected Writings*, XVII, and Susan Howson, ' "A Dear Money Man"? : Keynes on Monetary Policy, 1920', *Economic Journal*, LXXXII (2), June 1973.

74. 'Democracy and Efficiency', p. 123; see also *Collected Writings*, VII, pp. 379–81.

75. *Collected Writings*, IX, p. 331.

76. 'Art and the State – I', *The Listener*, 26 August 1936, p. 374 (reprinted above, p. 39). This broadcast contained a condemnation of raising the economic in unwanted places which deserves repeating, despite Mr White's earlier quotation (p. 23 above) from it :

> The [nineteenth century] view was the utilitarian and economic – one might almost say financial – ideal ... Bread and nothing but bread, and not even bread, and bread accumulating at compound interest until it has turned to stone ... We still apply some frantic perversion of business arithmetic in order to settle the problem whether it pays better to pour milk down drains or feed it to school-children. One form alone of uncalculated expenditure survives from the heroic age – War. And even that must sometimes pretend to be economic.

77. For example, Keynes's tendency towards rather wild asides, both in conversation and his more formal writing – e.g. the suggestion that 'by far the largest proportion of the world's greatest writers and artists have flourished in the atmosphere of buoyancy, exhilaration and the freedom from economic cares felt by the governing class, which is engendered by profit inflations' (*Collected Writings*, VI, p. 137 n.) – has gone undiscussed. Similarly his delight in words for their own sake has been left to speak for itself.

THE POLITICAL CONSEQUENCES OF LORD KEYNES
Roger Opie

It is conventional to say how pleased one is to be wherever one is, and I am in fact unconventionally pleased to be here today, and indeed honoured to join this quartet. The other three speakers are immersed in their knowledge of Keynes himself as a person and, in Dr Moggridge's case, all his papers. They faced problems of condensing all they knew into short papers. I fortunately had no such problems whatever: I just wrote and wrote all I could think. As a consequence I feel rather like Ringo joining the Beatles when the show was already on the road. I feel as though I might be the percussion section as it were – after the soft lyrics of Sir Roy, the dulcet tones of Mr White and the motown drawl of Dr Moggridge, now comes what you might call the heavy beat.

Keynes has had a profound, permanent, political impact in this country, throughout the English-speaking world, and indeed throughout Europe. This is neither surprising, nor unintended. In that famous and oft-quoted letter to G. B. Shaw, in 1935, he wrote, 'To understand my state of mind, however, you have to know that I believe myself to be writing a book on economic theory which will largely revolutionise – not, I suppose, at once, but in the course of the next 10 years – the way the world thinks about economic problems.' He was right. What is more, this was wholly in line with Keynes's view of what an economist should be. In the well-known passage in his biography of Alfred Marshall he spelt out his specifications of a first-class economist: 'He must be purposeful and disinterested in a simultaneous mood; as aloof and incorruptible as an artist yet sometimes as near the earth as a politician.'[1] That may not be exactly the posture all politicians adopt, but we know what he means. Keynes, whom Seymour Harris describes[2] as 'teacher, insurance executive, editor, college bursar, government servant, theatrical manager and prolific writer', was also, *because* he was all those things and more, a real politician as well. Indeed, his tactic at the height of the war, in scooping the Folger Library in Washington of a rare copy of an early edition of Spenser's *Faerie Queen* – he used the diplomatic bag to get an early sight of a catalogue – is worthy of any operator in the corridors of Westminster.

I want to divide what I have to say into three parts – first, the political consequences of Keynes's early writings; secondly, the consequences of his theories and thought; and, thirdly, the consequences of the policies and the economic behaviour which have followed from those theories.

It could be argued, I suppose, that Keynes caused the Second World War. That might be thought a slight exaggeration. And yet often in those bitter inter-war years, the Allied Powers might have acted to halt or at least frustrate Hitler's relentless drive to armed aggression. It was less a lack of power that made them hesitate and dither than a lack of moral confidence. The politicians and the public of the former Allies had no faith in the moral force of the Versailles Treaty, and found little appeal in the need to uphold it. The climate of opinion was such that confidence in the Settlement among the Allies was lowered, just as resentment at it within Germany was exacerbated.

There can be no doubt that Keynes's two books – *The Economic Consequences of the Peace* and *A Revision of the Treaty* – were most important factors in creating that intellectual, moral and political climate. The impact of the former book was of course enormous, it 'met with a reception which makes the word success sound commonplace and insipid'.[3]

As Keynes's obituary notice in *The Times* put it: 'His resignation from the British delegation to the Paris Peace Conference and his publication a few months later of the *Economic Consequences of the Peace* had immediate and lasting effects on world opinion about the peace treaty.' And opinion about that treaty soon became more important than the actual clauses of the Treaty.

Hitler was not slow, in his political appeals, both before and after he gained power, to exploit to the limit the moral and hence political vacuum which had at least partly been created by Keynes's writing. Indeed Hitler was perhaps the most fearsome example of those 'madmen in authority, who hear voices in the air ... distilling their frenzy from some academic scribbler of a few years back'.[4]

The inter-war situation is full of such paradoxes. There can be little doubt that if the level of unemployment in Germany had not risen so high, Hitler's Nazi Party would not have won so many frightened votes. But then, under the stimulus of militaristic and quasi-militaristic budgets, Hitler invented the *fact* of full employment about the same time as Keynes published the theory of it. If only the *General Theory* had preceded *The Economic Consequences of the Peace*!

But that is pure speculation. What is certain is Keynes's influence on the reparations settlement after the Second World War. He had persuaded the world that the budgetary and transfer problems of large-scale reparations out of current output were so formidable, or at least had been for the predominantly *laissez-faire* and deflation-prone economies of the 1920s, that post-1945 reparations to the Western Allies were made only from still-intact capital, and not from income. The Russians were not so inhibited in their Occupation Zone and took reparations from both!

Again it is amusing, if rather futile, to speculate. The economic foundations for the West German so-called 'economic miracle' were laid in the years when old capital equipment lost through destruction or reparation was being replaced by brand-new technology capital financed by Marshall Aid. What, one wonders, would have been the balance of economic and political power in Western Europe today if, instead, the West German economy had had to bear current reparations as burdensome as the continuing defence programme of the U.K.? There could, after all, have been no serious 'transfer problem' once Keynesian full-employment policies had been implemented.

But all that is the history of 'might-have-beens', of 'make-believe'. I want now to turn to the more positive political consequences of the later Keynes, of the *General Theory* and of the policies that flowed from it. This theory and an explosive growth of derivative ideas and insights were soon to be called the 'Keynesian Revolution'. If 'the Keynesian Revolution is a synonym for the New Economics',[5] is it also *the foundation of a New Politics*? I believe it is.

There is neither need nor time here to rehearse the main tenets of Keynesian economics. The key element is the analysis of under-employment equilibrium, with its corollary, the responsibility of government to attain and maintain full employment. In spite of the title of an earlier essay published in 1926, it was the *General Theory* of 1936 that signalled the true 'End of Laissez-Faire'. For this was a major attack on the central tenet of *laissez-faire* philosophy, *viz.* that there exists an essential harmony of economic forces, whose beneficent untrammelled working maximises the welfare of all. It could, of course, be admitted that there might be minor and temporary departures from this best of all possible worlds, but if so, they called simply for minor tinkering, for a screwdriver or some sticky tape, rather than for the design and creation of a completely new system. Keynes's central proposition was much more devastating. It was not simply the anarchic view that the level of output, employment and income might be anywhere, including at full employment, but the revolutionary view that *equilibrating* forces might establish that level anywhere and *keep it there*. If nothing positive were done, if *laissez-faire* prevailed, nothing would change.

The policy implication was simply that there had to be a policy, a governmental policy to shift the economy out of its under-employment position. But even that was not all. If eternal vigilance is the price of freedom, continuing action is the price of full employment. The Government would have to be continually active, because full employment, whether reached by accident or by positive policies, was a fragile condition. It could be maintained only so long as the volume of investment was high enough to offset the full employment level of savings. But that level of savings would be large, because saving was a function of income and income would be high; and also because unequal distribution of income at any given level of income promoted saving rather than consumption. Hence it could be argued that at any given level of income economic inequality was a drag on expansion, and made full employment highly vulnerable. Saving, and the economic argument for inequality based on the need for high savings, were thus turned upside down. '*Laissez-faire* made private vice into public virtue. The *General Theory* made private virtue into public vice.'[6] 'The old idea that equality and progress are incompatible is transformed by Keynes's theory into the revolutionary doctrine that greater equality is one of the essential conditions of progress.'[7]

This could be the basis of a radical programme if Keynes had wanted to make it so. Certainly all Keynesians in the early days and most Keynesians later on were radical in some sense or other, and few would have shrunk from the egalitarian implications of this analysis. But Keynes himself pushed for another policy to maintain full employment in a high-savings society. This was the greater socialisation of investment, in the face of getting interest rates low enough to provide a permanent stimulus, or low enough to offset a fall in private investment. This may have seemed to some to attack the fundamentals of the private sector, and hence to some to be very attractive. To Keynes, however, it was the lesser by far of the two evils. Better to lose the shadow of economic liberty if the price be the substance of economic prosperity.

But a high propensity to save was only one of the defects of *laissez-faire* economics. The second was the great difficulty in lowering interest rates enough. The obstacle here was not the need to stimulate sufficient saving – quite the contrary – but the income expectations of the rentier. Keynes viewed with equanimity, indeed with a certain glee, the euthanasia of the rentier as a necessary sacrifice in releasing the energies of the creators of wealth. Thus we have two 'fundamental' causes of unemployment, an attack on either of which, let alone on both, were treason to Keynes's class, and fairly radical.

Others apart from rentiers may also have felt threatened by the very tone of the *General Theory*. 'Keynes in the *Treatise* felt himself to be treading old ground in a somewhat different way: in the *General Theory*, he felt himself to be breaking quite new ground. The *Treatise* is written with serenity, the *General Theory* is up in arms.'[8] In this, Keynes simply reflected the temper of the times, and the shattering of earlier complacency. As Shackle puts it, the age of serenity, of tranquillity, of certainty, the belief in self-adjusting smoothly-working automatic economic forces was destroyed by outside events. The *General Theory* was both its obituary and a prospectus for a new world. But this new world would be one of uncertainty; of imperfect knowledge; of the necessary and continuous exercise of human judgement, in the pursuit not of some notional but natural optimum equilibrium position, but of the best we could do. A world of active, interventionist policy, of ad-hockery, of gadgetry.

But all this was to take place *within* the framework of the existing political and social order. It was not a call-to-arms to overthrow capitalist society, however aesthetically or morally repellent such a society might be. For such a society does at least deliver the goods. But it cannot guarantee full employment. Once that trifling defect is eliminated – and it *can* be without revolution – capitalist democracy offers the best hope of political freedom and economic prosperity. However radical and exciting or dangerous and threatening Keynesian theory may have seemed to some, others saw it as essentially the conservative programme of a liberal mind – as it was intended to be. Dillard puts it:

> Liberalism as a habit of mind tends to impute evil to wrong thinking rather than to irreconcilable conflicts embedded in the structure of society. . . .
> So we find Keynes always ready with a plan, a compromise or an amendment for resolving the problem at hand.[9]

A politically important by-product of attributing unemployment in a *laissez-faire* economy to the level of saving and the rate of interest was to declare other economic entities innocent. Keynes pardoned individual businessmen acting rationally in pursuit of their own interest – it was no part of *their* job to guarantee full employment, nor was it in their power. Just as important, Keynes exonerated the trade unions. Unemployment is not high because wages are too high – or for that matter too low. Wages are whatever they are, and so *prices* are what they are, but unemployment depends on the level of total demand. Wage cuts alone will not cure unemployment, nor do wage increases cause it. In passing, one might note an extraordinary revival of this wage-cut doctrine in the pronouncements of Her Majesty's present Ministers. We have been told frequently that the record levels of un-employment were due to the record rate of price inflation, and that in turn is due to the record rate of wage inflation. The implication was not that wage cuts would restore full employment – that would no doubt be a little too crude – but a much more subtle 'first derivative' argument, *viz.* that a cut in the rate of wage *increases* will do the trick. We have, fortunately, heard less of this antediluvian argument since Mr Barber's latest expansionary budget, and I expect we shall now hear no more of it at all.

Keynes's *General Theory* was radical enough, even if his philosophy was far from radical in any traditional sense. In-deed, he saw the *General Theory* as 'moderately conservative in its implications'.[10] For one who was so rude about Marx, Marxism and the readability of *Das Kapital*, it is delightful to reflect that Keynes filled exactly Marx's injunction to philosophers: 'The philosophers have only interpreted the world in various ways. The point, however, is to change it.'[11] He did more than that – he revolutionised it. The centre of the revolution is, of course, the achievement and the main-tenance of full employment in the post-war Western world. This has transformed, as it seems to me, the whole of political and social life, as much as and because it has transformed economic performance.

Some would argue that Keynesian policies had their first outing in Roosevelt's New Deal of the 1930s. I would doubt that, certainly if it is suggested that Keynesian ideas formed the basis of a coherent overall strategy. 'The policies of the President and his early advisers were indeed largely of the shot-gun variety.'[12] Not is it in the slightest degree true that full employment in Nazi Germany owed anything to Keynes-ian doctrine. Indeed, it seems probable that no German economist of the day would even read Keynes and certain that no German minister had. But the fact that the Nazis did pro-duce full employment had some important post-war political consequences. The only direct acquaintance that the German academic and intellectual world had with Keynes was his delivery of a lecture in Berlin, in 1926, entitled 'The End of Laissez-faire'. It was only too easy to believe that he actually *advocated* it. Then immediately after the war one of the first books to be translated which analysed Keynesian policies was *The Economics of Full Employment*[13] written by a number of economists at Oxford, all but one of them of recent Continental origin. That fact alone might have made Keynesians more attractive to German liberal opinion. It was no doubt inevitable, and it was certainly unfortunate, that the only example of full employment which was discussed, although explicitly *not* advocated, in that book was that of Nazi Germany. These two books retarded the development of Keynesian analysis and policies in Western Germany until a new post-war generation of graduates, many trained in the U.S., had gained position and power.

But to return to home ground. There are many who have attributed full employment in the U.K. since the war to Keynesian policy, and in particular to the intellectual victory Keynes won in converting the Treasury mandarins to his way of thinking. Certainly the famous closing paragraph of his *General Theory* suggests that he might thus have interpreted history, if someone in the heaven to which economists go had told him of the last twenty-six years. But I have always doubted that strict interpretation. My acquaintance with the Treasury Knights of all but the latest vintage, to say nothing of the central banking fraternity since 1694, suggests to me simply that they can, and do, use Keynesian terminology and even Keynesian tools in the pursuit of wholly anti-Keynesian policies.[14] For 'if Keynes can be said to have devoted his life to anything, it is to liberating internal policy from the domination of external factors'.[15] All too often have we seen instead 'the spectre of Lord Norman walking Westminster's battlements, tediously lecturing his countrymen on the need to create as much unemployment and as much business recession as might be required to check and reverse adverse balances in Britain's trading accounts'.[16] And no sooner did we at last achieve a large, if temporary external surplus, by means of devaluation and deflation, than another old doctrine was resurrected to take its place, *viz.* we must have high enough employment to stabilise prices. Keynesian language, Keynesian methods, but hardly Keynesian purposes.

I believe, instead, that far from creating full employment

in pursuit of a conscious social and political purpose, we simply inherited it from the war, and have (broadly) managed to retain it.[17] This is, in itself, no mean success, of course, and it is from that success that the political consequences of Keynes's life and work flow.

The first derives from the discovery that *maintaining* full employment requires the *ceaseless* management of the economy. This in turn creates ceaseless political tension in both Whitehall and Westminster. The practical question is how much to intervene, and in what way, in the workings of the private sector. There is, needless to say, endless pressure on Ministers and officials to minimise intervention (or interference, as it is usually called). We have thus seen a frantic search for tools that still fit a basically non-interventionist, indeed anti-interventionist, philosophy. The first, and crudest, was *pump-priming*, a one-shot injection of public spending. Then came the emphasis on, and creation of, *built-in stabilisers* – altering the *structure* of the economy by e.g. progressive tax rates and welfare benefits so that the limits of aberration are narrowed. Then came *automatic flexibility* – a flexible Bank Rate and a flexible exchange rate to achieve, miraculously, stable output, stable employment, stable prices and a stable external balance all at once. And finally, the *total automatism* of a rigid rate of growth of the money supply. No one, I suppose, would argue that all of these have been total failures – that what Andrew Shonfield[18] has called *neo-Keynesian laissez-faire* (or, in English, 'arm's-length government') has achieved nothing. But it has not had the success endlessly predicted by its proponents. However, each flirtation with automaticity soon leads to disillusion, to be followed by a hasty *ad hoc* retreat to direct detailed intervention – prices and incomes policies, national plans, direct controls. Even this hybrid version of *laissez-faire* works better than *laissez-faire* pure and simple. But interventionism is an ever-rising tide – it is rarely possible to have a 'bonfire of controls', and even deeply conservative governments, in the U.K., the U.S., Western Europe and Australasia, soon find themselves tempted to forget the principles on which they were elected to office – and to intervene.

Not only is there so little difference, for the man in the

street, between the stated intentions of Socialists and the
actions of Tories – that is bad enough. But the political dice
are inevitably loaded in favour of the Conservatives in managing the economy. Socialists interfere on principle, Conservatives out of necessity: Socialists out of malice, but
Conservatives out of sympathy. The business community will
naturally tolerate, and co-operate with, any policy imposed
by a party with which they are in basic sympathy, even though
they are wholly antipathetic to such a policy on principle.
The basic political fact of latent and mutual hostility between
Social Democrats (or in the U.S., just Democrats) and the
business community is bound to make economic management
at high levels of employment more difficult for Social Democratic Ministers, and hence to make electoral victories rare,
and electoral defeats frequent. Thus we have socialistic intervention imposed by Conservative Governments in pursuit of
a radical goal – that is real political compromise, real consensus politics. Keynes would have been amused.

In the process, two other significant changes have occurred
– everything economic or technical has been made political,
and politics has been made technical. In pre-Keynesian days,
many believed, or could be persuaded to believe, that unemployment was natural, and hence inevitable; business cycles
were natural; wages and prices were natural. Those few
economic elements which clearly were not, such as the gold
price, or Bank Rate, were purely technical and therefore no
business of ordinary mortals. Happily, those days are long past.
Now, it is acknowledged by all that the Government has both
the responsibility and the power to maintain full employment.
Hence unemployment becomes *politically* intolerable. And
the means to full employment become political – via higher
investment, *or* higher consumption, *or* higher government
spending. The choice matters a lot to a lot of people – and
the choice is not, or not wholly, technical. It is, at least in
part, purely political.

On the other side, politics has become much more technical.
Parties are elected on their promises to manage the economy
better than their opponents have done, or can be expected to
do, and are defeated largely, if not wholly, on the success
or failure of their economic management. *This* becomes the

yardstick of a party's claim to office.

The political debate centres on forecasts and projections, on tools and techniques, on means and not on ends. Not what sort of a society do we want, but how well can we manage the one that we have? No wonder that some economists would argue that 'full employment has become a right-wing slogan'.[19]

This is no doubt inevitable, if only because the need to manage the economy shifts the political struggle into the hands of the most conservative element in the whole political process, *viz.* the permanent Civil Service. They are never in office or out of it, but they are always in power; wholly non-political and yet at the centre of decision-making. As one of them once said, 'We have no time for politics – we're far too busy running the country.' This sinister shift of power has imposed a dreadful continuity of policy on the economy with crisis succeeding crisis, even though we have failed to achieve any major goal of economic policy. For some twenty years from VE-Day, we could at least claim that we had maintained employment at a higher level than Beveridge or Keynes ever foresaw. Keynes indeed wrote to Beveridge saying: 'No harm in aiming at 3 per cent unemployment, but I shall be surprised if we succeed.'[20] But now, since 1966, even that has been thrown to one side, in the frantic, misguided – and vain – pursuit of a strong balance of payments and stable prices!

The pursuit of full employment has inevitably enlarged greatly and permanently the active role of the State. But nothing succeeds like success. Public opinion soon, and inevitably, begins to ask what *else* the State may achieve in areas where private affluence alone is insufficient. Into area after area, the State is pushed or invited, omnipotent, benevolent, beneficent – in housing and slum clearance, in health, in education, in traffic engineering and in pollution.

This *ought* to mean that politics should again become political. 'Once the principle has been established that maintaining employment is a *public* concern, the question of what the employment shall be *for* becomes a political issue.'[21] Thus although the means towards full employment have produced 'consensus politics' – Butskellism as *The Economist* newspaper called it in the 1950s – the fact of full employment ought to have politicised every area of economic life. Politics is about choice, about priorities – about ends, not means. Full employment, working to capacity, brings choice back into the centre of the political arena. 'Economics becomes once more political economy. The *General Theory* brought out into the open the problems of choice and judgement that neo-classicals had managed to smother. There is no automatic re-conciliation of conflicting interests into a harmonious whole.'[22]

Once we have full employment or even employment only as high as the Treasury believe we can afford, anything and everything is at the expense of something else. A particular consequence is the changed nature of poverty. In the thirties, we had the infamous spectacle of poverty in the midst of plenty – but the plenty was purely potential. Now we have the scandal of poverty in the midst of *actual* plenty. Full employ-ment has not eliminated poverty. But whereas in the '30s all could have been winners and none need be losers – all could have been richer and none made poorer – the relief of poverty now requires *redistribution* out of a given total income. The poor can be made richer, but only if the richer can be, and are, made poorer. Once again, therefore, in curing the prob-lem of poverty, the technical and political are drawn tighter together.

This is, however, but one aspect of a much wider Keynesian consequence. Once we have full employment, anything and everything is at the expense of something else. The classical problem of scarce resources returns – and alas with it has come the revival of neo-classical economics, at least for the present. But while this bitter burden will no doubt pass, the former will remain. And this will make the ancient problems of the distribution of wealth and income the major economic, political and social problems of the next decade and more. Here lies the core of cost–push inflation, as managers, trade unionists and the non-unionised all struggle endlessly to in-crease or at least preserve their share of the national product.

There are some who believe that full employment and Keynesian policies to achieve it have created the problem of inflation, or at least made it insoluble. But I do not for one moment agree with, e.g., Professor Johnson,[23] who argues that as a result of full employment, governments have lost control of money wages and prices. For that implies that if there were

unemployment governments *would* have control. Some economists may believe that the Phillips curve once encircled
the British economy in its grip – none can surely believe it
now. It is not current full employment that produces this
dread outcome – but the *experience* of *past* high employment
which has given unions the taste of power; and the combination of organised labour and oligopolised industry which has
given them the opportunity to exercise it without limit.
Hence, whatever control governments or central banks may
once have had, indirectly, over wages and prices, through
their willingness to deflate the economy, that control or influence has now been torn apart and shown to be a sham. It
cannot be regained by short sharp bursts of deflation, or even
by prolonged unemployment. The best hope of more stable
prices now lies in yet more politicising of economic cate-
gories – of prices, dividends, charges, rents and wages[24] (what
is called 'incomes and prices policy') and an acceleration of
growth towards higher employment.

Even so, high employment has no doubt exacerbated the
problem of inflation. Certainly this was the expectation of
Keynesians very early on. In the *General Theory*, inflation is
very simple – as demand increases up to full employment, output rises: beyond full employment, prices rise. In the real
world, it is more complex. If you expand, you get inflation
before full employment; if you contract, you get unemployment before stable prices.[25] This has led, at least in part, to
the agonising and agonised swings of policy known as 'stop-
go'. But 'stop-go' is only in part an economic phenomenon –
it is much more a political one. For the *trade* cycle has given
way to the *electoral* cycle. Nature has given way to artefact.

But the authorities have now been caught out. The British
public at least have learnt a lot about Keynesian economics.
They have learnt in particular to forecast the direction of
changes in indirect taxes, or in the availability of credit, and
to hedge. In advance of an expectedly tough budget, they
step up their purchases, and if the budget is expected to be
expansionary, they postpone them. Consumer behaviour can
no longer be econometrically forecast from income data alone,
or from any other model based on stable past relationships.[26]
Thus consumers have joined businessmen in an ancient sport

long played in the government bond market – the only way to prosper is not to calculate genuine objective long-term prospects, but to guess what the Government is going to do next before it does it. Such behaviour in the bond market affects no one outside it – but in the goods markets it affects all of us directly as well as the next stage of government policy. Macro-economic policy is now operating within a system which *sometimes* has positive feedback – but not always. Such an environment, born out of repeated and bitter experience, can only make such policy-making even more difficult, and less likely to succeed.

Some economists[27] argue that, faced with a choice of full employment or stable prices, governments have taken a calculated risk and settled for inflation rather than unemployment. Even if that were the straight and only choice, I would settle for full employment every time, unless the inflation was really severe. But it is not the *only* choice, unless one believes that there is no way of breaking a presumed tight link between the level of employment and the rate of inflation, no way of shifting a presumed Phillips curve. I believe there is a way – but that involves still more political intervention in the wage-setting and price-fixing processes.

Whether or not full employment causes incomes and prices to rise fast, or only permits them to do so, there is little doubt that Keynes would have viewed the prospect of creeping inflation with dismay. 'Lenin was certainly right. There is no subtler, no surer means of overturning the existing basis of society than to debauch the currency.'[28] Lenin argued thus and favoured it – Keynes agreed and feared it. It is a silly slander to suggest that Keynesian economics is inflationary by definition.

One very good reason why Keynes would surely have disapproved of the inflation which we have experienced in the last decade is the unfortunate but inevitable sociological by-product of the public's growing consciousness of rising prices. Whereas full employment and higher real incomes are said by some sociologists to have led to the 'bourgeoisification of the proletariat' there is much evidence that inflation, and concern over money incomes, has led to the 'proletarianisation of the bourgeoisie'. The middle-class professions have made great strides in building defences against erosion of their living standards, even to the extent that doctors and teachers have gone or threatened to go on strike. Such behaviour would have been unthinkable, and unnecessary, in the days of high unemployment and stable prices – all that was necessary then was the creation of professional associations and the policing of professional standards, both highly respectable activities. Inflation hath made bullies of us all.

And *that*, if it continues, could have frightening consequences for the tolerance and good humour of British political life.

Before I finish, I ought to admit that I have said nothing about the international side, partly because I think that would make a very good set of lectures for the second of these seminars. All that I would say now is that it does seem to me that one of the unfortunate by-products of Keynesian policy has been to re-promote some people I'd always thought had been effectively demoted, *viz.* the central bankers of the world. One of the minor benefits of full employment policies as envisaged by Keynes was to place Treasury ministers firmly on the top of the central bankers. After all, Treasury ministers are directly responsible to Parliament. But concentration on national domestic equilibrium has made international disequilibrium more likely; and because it narrows the room for manoeuvre – governments can no longer simply deflate the economy by 10 or 20 per cent to restore the balance of payments – external disequilibrium both becomes more difficult to deal with, and seems to be a largely monetary phenomenon. And then, of course, the central bankers of the world come back into the foreground, to reclaim and regain this lost territory. Very unfortunate.

The most important political consequence of Keynes's life and work seems to me to have been the rebirth of political economy – the reintegration of political social and economic life. This is a consequence I wholly welcome, not least for the effect it has on economists. If it is part of the ethics of medicine to examine and stress the side-effects and by-products of their work, it is no less part of the professional ethics of economists to do the same. Political economy can thus make economists human beings once more.

NOTES

1. J. M. Keynes, *Essays in Biography* (London: Macmillan, 1972), p. 174.

2. S. E. Harris, *The New Economics* (London: Dobson, 1948), p. 59.

3. J. A. Schumpeter, *Ten Great Economists* (London: Allen & Unwin, 1952), p. 266.

4. J. M. Keynes, *The General Theory of Employment, Interest and Money* (London: Macmillan, 1973), p. 383.

5. D. Dillard, *The Economics of J. M. Keynes* (London: Crosby Lockwood, 1948), p. xiii.

6. Joan Robinson, *Economic Philosophy* (London: C. A. Watts, 1962), p. 75.

7. Dillard, *The Economics of J. M. Keynes*, p. 331.

8. G. L. S. Shackle, *The Years of High Theory* (Cambridge: Cambridge University Press, 1967), p. 295.

9. Dillard, *The Economics of J. M. Keynes*, p. 301.

10. Keynes, *General Theory*, p. 377.

11. K. Marx, *Theses on Feuerbach* (1845).

12. Harris, *The New Economics*, p. 18.

13. Oxford: Basil Blackwell, 1945, ed. F. Burchardt.

14. I am encouraged in this heresy by the writings of Sir Roy Harrod, e.g., *Towards a New Economic Policy* (Manchester: Manchester University Press, 1969).

15. R. F. Kahn in *Selected Essays on Employment and Growth* (Cambridge: Cambridge University Press, 1973), p. 113.

16. R. Lekachman, *The Age of Keynes* (London: Penguin, 1969), p. 226.

17. See, e.g., R. C. O. Matthews, 'Why Britain has had Full Employment since the War', *Economic Journal*, September 1968.

18. In *Modern Capitalism* (London: Oxford University Press, 1965).

19. Robinson, *Economic Philosophy*, p. 95.

20. Kahn, *Essays on Employment and Growth*, p. 98.

21. Robinson, *Economic Philosophy* (Watts), p. 97.

22. Ibid., p. 76.

23. In *Inflation and the Monetarist Controversy* (Amsterdam: North Holland, 1972), p. 11.

24. See, e.g., F. Blackaby in *New Society*, 9 November 1972.

25. See, e.g., Lekachman, *The Age of Keynes*, p. 125.

26. See, e.g., L. R. Klein, *The Keynesian Revolution* (London: Macmillan, 2nd edition, 1967), p. 203.

27. E.g., Johnson, *Inflation and the Monetarist Controversy*, pp. 11–12.

28. J. M. Keynes, *The Economic Consequences of the Peace* (London: Macmillan, 1971), p. 149.

Mr Michael Stewart: I agree with what Roger Opie said about income distribution as perhaps the coming thing. There will be great attention paid to this during the next decade or so. I think this is also true of income distribution on a global scale, although Mr Opie was concerned about income distribution within this country. But I think on a global scale we also have to think of this as a problem for at least the rest of the century, and this is why I was interested in an essay Dr Moggridge mentioned, 'Economic Possibilities for our Grandchildren', written, I suppose, about forty years ago. In a way it has not so far proved a very prescient essay. Keynes talked in that essay, as I recall, about the solving of the economic problem and he looked forward to a world in which the kind of activities that Mr White was talking about earlier on, would flourish: we would all be happy listening to music and painting paintings – the economic problem would have taken care of itself. Clearly this is very much not the case, although we're 40 per cent of the way to the year 2030 that Keynes was thinking of. This is perhaps because he overestimated technical progress, and underestimated the ability of the advertising industry, and of manufacturing industry generally, to persuade us all that we should have more and more of the fruits of technical progress. He was not concerned with what we're increasingly told are the finite limits of the planet. Now if you put these two things together and you have increasing production of goods, increasingly sophisticated goods in the Western economies, which everybody feels they have to have, with the finite nature of the planet, then you get not only this problem of income distribution *within* countries, but also this problem of income distribution between countries. I think one's outlook for the next sixty years of Keynes's 100 years is perhaps rather gloomy.

Now this, I think, does lead one to agree with Roger Opie when he says what we need perhaps is a move back to political economy, to a kind of economics which takes increasing account of political and social factors and gets away from the more dry, arid, kind of model-building which we've seen a lot of during the last twenty years. I think that if there is such a move back, Keynes – if he were still with us – would probably be the first to welcome it.

Mrs Margaret Gowing: I would like to take up this point that applies to both speakers. Mr Opie said full employment was in effect a hangover from the war. Presumably he means by this that it was partly the continuing defence commitment – is not that part of the argument?

Roger Opie: Very little.

Mrs Gowing: I wonder whether I could take it up though. I think it is surprising, taking up his point that economists need to be political economists, that in fact, for example, we have had no economic analysis of the impact of defence, either on the internal economy of this country or, indeed, on the international economy, when it has been one of the major factors in the economic life of the last twenty-five years. But I wonder, if one assumes that in fact defence has had a greater impact on the post-war economy, whether Dr Moggridge can say whether in going through Keynes's papers he has found very much evidence that Keynes was aware of this? – because, if one goes back to *How to Pay for the War*, indeed, to the scheme for post-war credits, and all the papers I saw when I was a Civil Servant during the war doing post-war reconstruction, there was the assumption that there was going to be deficient demand after the war. But I certainly never saw anywhere an assumption that there was going to be a continuing and high defence commitment. I wonder if there is material in Keynes's papers to show that he was aware of the possibilities?

Dr D. E. Moggridge: The evidence, in a way, is rather ambiguous. From what I can recollect, Keynes was not prone to assume that there would be deficient demand right after the war. Rather he thought that problem stood ten to fifteen years in the future. As for the possibility of a continuing high level of defence expenditure after the war keeping the level of aggregate demand up, the papers suggest that Keynes did not consider it. However, in the discussions of post-war reparations from Germany, Keynes did raise the alternative problem, when he suggested in a Treasury paper that Germany should be asked to contribute to keeping the post-war peace of the world, for, if she did not and could not spend on defence as a result of the peace treaty, she could be more successful in achieving a high rate of economic growth.

Mr Opie: In reply to Mrs Gowing, I didn't actually mean that, although I think obviously that that has been a major part of it. What I meant was that I think it was obviously much easier from a policy point of view to inherit the very large role of government which wartime had created, and the full employment which had gone with it; and then to bend political forces, political tools, economic tools to maintain it. One can imagine that the conversion – as it's called – of the civil service machine and politicians as a whole to the active pursuit of full employment in peacetime, without the war, would have been postponed *sine die.* The balance of payments, you see, could never stand it, and you can imagine that we would never have been able to pay the price of such affluence. So unless one had foreseen that somehow or other the United States (or other major countries) would have been converted I think we would never have been able to lead a move towards full employment because of sterling and all that sort of stuff that we know only too well and have come to live with and love. We would never have been able to lead – I doubt whether we would have been able to follow quite so easily; but having inherited this situation, and seen that it was possible (unemployment down to what? – one per cent) at the end of a very large State exercise in managing the economy, it was easy to maintain. And, fortunately, the outside world was, on the whole, highly prosperous, so the balance of payments wasn't a binding constraint – it was on occasions, as we know, but it wasn't one which prevented us getting below 10 per cent. That was really what I meant about inheriting it.

Mr Philip Mahr: Mr Opie mentioned Professor Shackle. Didn't he also argue that the publication of Professor Gunnar Myrdal's work *Monetary Equilibrium* anticipated the theoretical argument of the *General Theory* without getting any of the credit? Myrdal's book was published in Swedish and German in 1933 but in English only in 1939. On top of that, am

I right in thinking that Swedish politicians pursued conscious anti-unemployment policies in the early thirties and that it was probably the Swedes who led the application of soundly-based theories to these practical policies?

Mr Opie: I suppose that proves the great disadvantage of our having different languages. I accept that what you say may be true, I am no expert at all, you are the expert here and indeed out there. Whether it was true that the social democratic government in Sweden did pursue this sort of policy as a result of theoretical insight, or whether it was one of those lucky *ad hoc* situations – that I don't know at all. But language is a real problem – Kalecki is an example.

Professor M. J. C. Vile: Perhaps I could ask Mr Opie something which might provoke him to say something a bit more about the end of his talk, because, if I understood him correctly, he was arguing that governments ought to interfere much more, not just for the sake of attempting to gain a more equitable distribution of income, but because in the past they have wanted for one reason or another continually to go back to some sort of automatic mechanism which did not involve them in the detailed regulation or detailed intervention in economic life. Now many of us have a view of government that suggests that it is all too ready, when it can attempt to regulate things, to do so; and its reluctance to do so, whether it be a Labour or Conservative Government, seems on the face of it rather odd. If this is what he is proposing it seems to me to have political consequences which politicians are very well aware of, and it may be the reason why they flee back all the time to this kind of reliance upon automatic mechanisms. That is to say that the more the Government intervenes, and the more it intervenes in detail, the more unpopular it inevitably becomes, unless you assume that the Government is all-powerful, omniscient and will always be efficient in its interventions. Because inevitably in its interventions, although they may help some, although conceivably they may improve the whole situation, they will inevitably interfere with the lives and interests of individuals and groups in the community, and as such will bring down upon government a considerable amount of unpleasant comment, all the way through to active refusal to co-operate. It does seem to me that what Mr Opie was suggesting was a route which politicians in a democratic country are unlikely to want to take, because they realise only too well that this kind of intervention will lead to a particular government becoming unpopular – and the more its life goes on the more unpopular it becomes – but also perhaps they realise it will make government as such unpopular; and that, therefore, the more you've got to involve yourself in saying whether Mr A. shall get a certain amount of money and Mr B. shall get more or less money than Mr A., then the more you are going on a road which is going, sooner or later, either to make you impose this with force, or to be driven out of power. This is the basic political problem at the root of the economic problem; and it seemed to me that at the end of his talk at any rate, Mr Opie didn't give any indication of how effective he thought government intervention might be, and whether it could possibly avoid this potentially catastrophic effect upon democratic government.

Mr Opie: I must say that all sounds very frightening, I don't think I said that in my view governments ought to intervene – though I'm not horrified at the thought that they might do so, or that they do do so – not even simply in order to get a better distribution of income. What I was arguing was that, in order to maintain what we already have, it seems to me that with the way economic and political forces are evolving governments will have to be prepared continually to contemplate further intervention. Now I agree with Professor Vile that one of the major problems of intervention is that it is almost bound to be discriminatory; it is bound to affect some, or seem to affect some, more and some worse than others; and of course, those who are hurt will yell louder than those who benefit. The latter are the silent majority, I dare say, but the very non-silent, the very vocal minority will make a great deal of fuss, and, therefore, of course, governments must make certain that they only hurt their friends. Labour Governments must bash the trade unions; Conservative Governments must never bash trade unions, but must bash big business. That, of course, is the way to survive politically; you can always rely on your friends. It's the middle ground that is so difficult to win and that, of course, is what basically matters. I think the other reason why non-intervention is so popular is that the Civil Service, I believe, largely dislikes it – hates it. It sees it, quite rightly, as you are implying, as a certain way of getting their Minister in trouble, and one of the marks of a good year's administration is that you kept your Minister out of trouble – that he never had any difficult questions to answer (even unrigged questions that were never very difficult to answer). It may be that the true monopoly profit is a quiet life. Well, the virtue of a whole year's good administration is again a quiet life. So that Civil Servants are, I believe, very much opposed to intervention – I don't think on grounds of *laissez-faire* philosophy – but on grounds of their own position. Nonetheless, I do believe that there will be this continuing tension. I don't know – how can one know? – whether this will be an ever-rising tide, swamping party after party and group after group, and whether we will then land up in a corporate state. If so I object, as it were – I don't wish to land up in a corporate state; but I'm just simply saying that it seems to me a very likely outcome of the way in which political economy and political life and economic life are developing. Whether the democratic processes are strong enough to stand up to that, I suppose, is another issue, but I would have imagined so. Do people feel that Sweden is a non-interventionist society? I don't know. But do they feel that it is a highly totalitarian society? They don't. Now there are of course some dissident groups, and there are students who break up universities, and there's a high suicide rate, alcoholism and so on and so forth. Well, I'm against all those things on the whole, but I don't regard them as a terrible deprivation of freedom, and a terrible destruction of democratic processes or even of democracy itself. So I would have thought that there isn't an inevitability about this; but of course there is clearly a great danger, and I suppose, again, eternal vigilance is what one wants.

Professor D. Lockard: At the end of Mr Opie's remarks he said that in the thirties there was less opportunity, that is to say that there was then a potential for greater good for all but it wasn't developed, I assume because of the depression. Are you suggesting that at the present time there is not an opportunity for expansion and for development; and if so, is that for reasons of exhaustion of resources or some other point?

Mr Opie: The answer is, I suppose, no, I was not suggesting that. I was simply contrasting, if you like, the basic situation which has ruled in this country, on the whole, since 1945, of unemployment down below 2 per cent. Therefore, if you are to do a great good to one group of society, it has to be at the cost of higher taxes, or what have you, on another group, and that there isn't more for all at any given moment. That is why politicians are so desperate to get faster growth. That then breaks this confine and simply says that all can have more and each can have more at the expense of no one else; the actual gain of each is only at the cost of a potential greater gain for others, but none need actually lose. That, of course, is why politicians love growth; they seldom achieve it, but they love it. Now, at the moment, of course, there is plenty of such potential; but if and when the economy returns to full employment, then we are back in this classical problem that everything is at the expense of something else. That was really what my point was.

Dr J. L. Carr: Somebody referred to Keynes's remark about the euthanasia of the rentier; and I would like to ask what people think of this, because it seems to me that it is open to a good deal of misunderstanding and that misunderstanding has done a great deal of harm to what advertisers would call the Keynesian image, and got them this reputation of being inflationists. Now what Keynes meant, I feel fairly sure, was that interest rates would fall to low levels. He did not, I think, envisage negative interest rates, though he did have a few remarks about stamped money and other such novelties. But what has happened, of course, since the war is that interest rates on fixed securities over long periods have been negative in real terms. Anyone who was rash enough to buy War Loan at par during the war, and has held on to it ever since, has today got about 37 (or is it 38?) 1972 pounds, in exchange for 100 1942 pounds as it might have been, and his interest at about 50s a year after tax on £100 worth pays maybe about as much as 10s a year would have bought when he put the money up. Now what seems to me alarming about this from a social point of view is that it is predominantly small savings that are invested in fixed-interest savings deposits and securities that are being eroded, while richer people, particularly those who were big landowners and urban landowners, have done extremely well out of the inflationary process, which has thus accentuated inequality in the ownership of property. The other disadvantage of a negative and uncertain interest rate seems to me nothing to do with the distribution of income, but the fact is that for anyone, whoever you are, it is impossible to redistribute your income through time with any confidence: if you save money you may, and probably will, lose by it. And the effects of unnecessary consumption, not to mention pollution and exhaustion of natural resources and all that, of a built-in incentive to spend your money on goods or something when you get it, rather than save it, seem to me very serious. I haven't heard much criticism of our current inflationary way of life from this point of view.

Mr Opie: I agree with the implication that it is a scandal that small savers are unable to protect the real value of their savings. I wonder how many schemes to make this possible have been put up by the permanent Civil Servants to Chancellors and turned down. There are plenty of schemes to protect investors in the City, but not many that *we*'ve heard of – of course, there was the Premium Bond scheme and occasionally there are suggestions of higher rates on new issues of National Savings Certificates, but nothing really spectacular. Now it ought to be possible, I would have thought, with the infinite ingenuity of Civil Servants, to devise schemes which don't run into the great problem of an enormous amount of switching from existing savings, and which would give the small saver a chance of keeping ahead – that is to say, to have protective areas of high-yield savings, if this is thought to be desirable. I think it is, because I think it is monstrously unfair obviously, that only the rich – so to speak – can protect themselves against something which is going to impoverish all the rest. I'm not sure that I am in favour of high interest rates across the board to achieve this. (In fact if anything I suppose I'm temperamentally a low-interest rate man, but that is no doubt oldfashioned, and derives from my childhood, perhaps.) But if that cannot be done, if it is not possible to devise clever, localised schemes, then I think the demotion of interest rates as an important weapon could safely mean higher interest rates than we have seen in money terms for a long time. But the other technique, of course, would be to slow down the rate of inflation. I suppose that would do it at a stroke (I might have said it if someone else hadn't said it before).

Professor Austin Robinson: I would like to ask Mr Vile whether, again, I may be allowed to come back to Keynes as a person – the things that Roy Harrod was talking about at the beginning, the things which Don Moggridge has been talking about. I've enjoyed myself enormously today because I have tried to write, I think, five times in my life about Keynes. I've been condemned by Milo Keynes to write the sixth time, but I have a difficulty – a blockage – in writing about Keynes. I always start with a determination to look at Keynes objectively – to regard him as no different from the rest of us, and to see whether I cannot bring him down to earth and make him as little distinguished as any other lecturer in any other lecture room. I always fail, because by about page 5 of my document – if not earlier – it becomes only too apparent that I regard Keynes as one of the few great men with whom I have ever worked or whom I have ever seen. I was lucky enough to spend most of my war inside the Cabinet Office in a very junior capacity, where one could see the great men at work, and by any standard by which I can measure people, Keynes was among the very few of the very great indeed.

I first saw Keynes in the autumn of 1919. I had come back from trying to fly aeroplanes in the war to trying to recover enough Latin and Greek to satisfy my College, who thought I ought to be earning my keep as a classical scholar, and finding it extremely difficult. I cut some lectures on Livy in order to go and hear Keynes give lectures on the economic consequences of the peace, and I can still picture him there in the lecture room as a young man. His burning indignation with the world, with the Treaty as it was working out, his care for the world, the sense of importance of things that he was conveying to us – these stick in my mind. Those few lectures made me decide that economics was my subject and not the classics.

But as a teacher – this I think was what Keynes communicated to his pupils in a most extraordinary way: his passionate concern about the things of the world. We learnt to be professional economists – if we did – at the feet of Pigou, of Dennis Robertson and others who were absolutely first-rate teachers. But we learnt something quite quite different from Keynes – that we had got to think about the world, we had got to care about the world; that if we were going to get the problems of the world straight we had got to do it by some hard fundamental thinking. And thirdly, and I find it terribly difficult to say it, we learnt a sort of conceit that if *we* were not going to think about the world, nobody else was going to think about the world. Now there's still a large element of truth in that. The number of people who are prepared to think fundamentally about the problems of the world, the economic problems of the world, are all too few and there is a duty on those who are capable of doing it to try to do this thinking. I agree entirely with what Don Moggridge has said on Keynes's own approach to these problems. He taught us to question and he always questioned himself.

I can think of no original piece of theoretical economics which Keynes conceived as an exercise in pure economics and not as part of the process of trying to think about how to get the world straight. Once he was faced with the problem of trying to get the world straight, he was prepared to go to all lengths to get this thinking right. This is what I think you are going to learn from the two fascinating books that Don Moggridge is at present engaged in finishing up and which we are going to be publishing for you at the end of March next – books which show how Keynes moved over a period of four years, from the first intuitions in thinking about the problems of under-employment and about getting the world straight in the conditions of 1930 to the final formulation of the *General Theory*. And what is immensely impressive is how much trouble Keynes took at that stage, with how much concentration he went on, not only with those of us who were living in Cambridge at the time, but with Roy Harrod, with Hawtrey, with all the others who were thinking and working with him, not least Dennis Robertson. With Dennis he parted brass rags in the final stages, but in the important formative stages Dennis and he were very close together indeed.

If I may go back to Maynard as a teacher, I think all of us who were near to him went through three phases. In the first phase, and this was particularly true of his undergraduate pupils, people were his uncritical admirers. They were dominated by him, and it was terribly easy to be dominated by him – we were all dominated by him. In the second stage our intellectual integrity, our intellectual honesty, made us want to escape from Maynard's domination, and almost all of us went through this phase of trying to escape. It was a sort of stage of intellectual puberty. Those who really grew up to be economists passed through this stage of intellectual puberty and grew back into admiration, into sympathy, into a capacity to work and agree with Keynes. But a surprising number in that generation of our friends and colleagues got stuck in the age of intellectual puberty and never escaped into adult life.

There's one final thing that I would like to say. Maynard taught us to question, to think for ourselves, to accept nothing and be absolutely ruthless when we tried to see our way through problems – to question, and question. Now I get rather frightened in this generation, and I hate it as much as I believe he would have hated it, when people, like preachers in a pulpit, start trying to preach a sermon (which nearly always says something entirely different) by beginning by quoting a text from the Holy Writ of Maynard. Maynard certainly never looked on the *General Theory* as his last word in economics. We've got (or Don Moggridge will be providing for you) the record, so to speak, the chapter headings, the skeleton of what he was meaning to go on to after the *General Theory*. But Maynard's intellectual development would not have stopped short at the *General Theory*; he had taught us how to go on and on and on thinking; and I believe that if he were here today what he'd be saying to you is: 'Forget the *General Theory*. That was a stage in the development of economics; it's not the last word in economics. Go on, and think for yourselves, and unless you are thinking for yourselves you're not doing your job as economists.'

Index

Compiled by Barbara Lowe